Weird Emptiness

Weird Emptiness

Essays & Aphorisms

Alex Stein

San Antonio, Texas
2007

Weird Emptiness: Essays & Aphorisms © 2007
by Alex Stein

Cover painting, "Pulse" © 2002 by Andrea Belag.
Courtesy of Mike Weiss Gallery, New York.

First Edition

ISBN-13: 978-0-916727-38-3

Wings Press
627 E. Guenther
San Antonio, Texas 78210
Phone/fax: (210) 271-7805
On-line catalogue and retail ordering:
www.wingspress.com
Wings Press is distributed by IPG
www.ipgbook.com

Library of Congress Cataloguing-in-Publication Data:

Stein, Alex, 1961-
  Weird emptiness : essays & aphorisms / Alex Stein. -- 1st ed.
    p. cm.
  ISBN 978-0-916727-38-3 (pbk. : alk. paper)
  I. Title.
  PS3569.T349W45 2007
  813'.54--dc22
                                        2007033345

Contents

Weird Emptiness

Essays & Aphorisms

Preface

I do not encourage anyone to write, and believe me it is not because I fear the competition. Writing clarifies nothing, except the still, bright light of paradox that shines above every enterprise, every experience, every idea. It is of no earthly use, unless one's secret desire is to become a worldless mendicant, and even then it is better bypassed in favor of self-abnegation and such deeds as at least have the virtue of achieving for others. However, if you must press on (this author, himself, did, you might be thinking, so perhaps all these perorations are mere jibber-jab) do so with a hard heart. Believe me, you will need it. And by hard, I do not mean nickel plated. If you don't understand why, just yet, you will soon enough. To get started you will need a writing implement, some blood, and an anvil or a block of granite against which to pound your forehead. The blood is for drinking. Faint-of-hearts may substitute red wine. The abstemious: water mumbled over by a priest. Penitents: bile. In any case, there must be something to wet the lips. It is dry work, extracting the marrow of idea from the bone of thought. Next: address yourself to some entity or other. Deity or dog, it hardly matters. What matters is to set your arrow upon a taut bow-string and draw it back. The riven target will rarely be that one upon which the writer had set his sights. Intention is just a means for getting started. All true ends are interior. The writer, if he is honest, will fell himself.

Maxim: The light you bring to bear upon your subject will flow from the wound of your own illumination. Prepare yourself to die a thousand deaths. The mind is a dark forest. A tangled thicket. Despise all guides. Cut your own path. Your words must be for you a sharp scythe.

The Book of Happiness

The Book of Happiness. The history of literature, at least as it could be told by its authors, is a history of the fear of happiness. Trace literature in any direction, to its roots or to its ends and that is practically all you will find: fear of happiness. Given the vast realm of happiness one would think that a book of happiness would occasionally be written. Oh, yes, perhaps you and I are put here on the earth with all the others to write the books of our happinesses.

Cervantes. Imagine a Miguel de Cervantes put here on earth to write the book of his happiness and imagine a Miguel de Cervantes who insists (but the judge at the gate is already beginning to scowl) that this monstrous *Don Quixote*, this illegitimate off-spring of terror and depression, this big bastard of a book . . . imagine a Miguel de Cervantes who insists that such a book *is* the book of his happiness . . . now imagine the depth of despair to which one must have at first been plunged to write a *Don Quixote* as one's prescription and as one's remedy.

Despair. One thinks of Soren Kierkegaard as despairing, but it is as simple as this to dispel that notion: despair is never aware of itself as despair. Always masquerading itself as something else, despair goes gaily to its gallows. Awareness to the gallows never goes, but despair every day from the gallows pole, swinging, peals forth its gales of laughter.

Suffering. One knows of Kierkegaard that he suffered, but for what or for whom? He suffered for his fate as the "one who knows," the "exception," the one "born reflective." Carrying the burden of all the history of folly that goes by the name of philosophy, Kierkegaard, like a reluctant mule, wrote terrifying words of transparency and towering works of redemption.

Kierkegaard's Daemon. Somewhere over Kierkegaard's shoulder was a daemon called Pseudonym. An oracular figure but absolutely the antithesis of, say, that noble Oracle at Delphi to whom Socrates historically adhered. This Pseudonym was a fervid creature so absorbed in his own marvelous confusion that the profligate son of destiny whom he attended was to him a mere bagatelle. However, does this impugn the character of Kierkegaard? What a bitter pill it must have been to swallow that soul (his own?) before entering into our world as the illuminated SK. Master Cervantes, did *you* at the gate of our world swallow the soul of your monstrous text? Master Cervantes, did you at the gate of our world swallow the variegate, bawdy soul that redounds through *Don Quixote* and is holy? Mayhem! Chaos! Did you really swallow all this in a draught as you entered through the gate?

Reflections on Meaning. The antithesis of this: SK's relentless reflections on meaning. His writing hand drawing succor from the well of emptiness. (But, what Kierkegaard and Cervantes mainly share is enormous lucidity, and allegorical instincts.)

Three Knights. Kierkegaard's Knight of Infinite Resignation. Cervantes' Knight of the Sad Face. Tennyson's Lancelot. Of which one was it said: "His broad clear brow in sunlight glowed"? Just as there is only one true faith, there is only one true knight. And just as that knight will never be named, that knight's quest will never be ended. (One might, at this time, think of Dostoyevsky's "first of a quadrillion steps in darkness." Less so of Lao Tzu's renowned dictum: "The journey of one thousand miles with a single step is begun." So, if it is with infinite resignation that we enter upon the eternal way, let it be at least with joyous countenance that we do so – that is to say let us have away with and stricken from our memories, if need be, Cervantes' grotesque; let us cleave to "the beautiful" as if it might lead us to "the just," since nothing else has, and since no amount of reasoning seems ever likely to bring us – to that "just" – any more close. One might with the same notion of "infinite resignation" launch a defense of *Don Quixote*, but *Don Quixote* does not need a defense, it needs a long, long rest, away from the prying eyes of every amateur history buff from Kafka to Foucault and away from the prying eyes of every amateur psychologist from Kierkegaard to Bakhtin.)

The Prologue. If there is any single final issuance or utterance with regard to *Don Quixote* (and whoever thinks so is a dunce) than there is a single final issuance or utterance to *every point and part of DQ*, and if there is that, then that single final issuance or utterance must be that it was writ to undermine authority. The authority of Chivalric tradition, obviously, but obviously, too, the authority of the text (and with/in that text, the authority of authorship). Whosoever would point out the flaws of the world and have his or her criticisms taken to heart, must first be able to point with relish to his or her own failings, and certainly to the failings of whatever is, has been or ever will be his or her medium. That's all the Prologue to *Don Quixote* is: a long self-scrutiny, the virtue of which is all in its comedy, the comedy of which is all in its tone, the tone of which is all in earnest. (So, too, was the famous dead-pan of silent film star Buster Keaton all in earnest, and for all the same reasons.)

The Knight of Infinite Signification. *Don Quixote* is entirely about its (each) individual reader, as far as I can figure anything. It is a long meditation on the analytical modalities of a life lived self-consciously. How is biography created? Autobiography? What is reason and reasoning? How can an authentic communication be achieved when no authoritative representation can be agreed upon: either with the big questions or with the small ones? That is why one might rightly call Don Quixote: The Knight of Infinite Signification.

The Other Thing. The other thing I notice about Don Quixote and about Sancho Panza is that each is absolutely filthy. There is a scene in which SP evacuates his bowels in close proximity to DQ, secretively, I already forget why, and he manages to get away with it, though it is a particularly foul bowel movement, and I notice that he is neither in a physical position, nor does it seem to be a pressing concern of his in any way, to wipe himself afterwards. I'm not sure that a character can live something like that down in the eyes of even a remotely healthy-minded reader.

The Truth about Don Quixote. *Don Quixote* is finally a critical and not a creative text. I do not mean our jaded epoch has made it come so before our eyes, I mean in and of itself. *DQ* is an ideological treatise before it is anything resembling a creative flourish. That, in its dogged prodigy, it does finally beg to be taken as a work of sheer inventiveness and imagination, does not in any way disprove my thesis. DQ begins in criticism. With a book burning. With the note of elegy sounding for a whole age as the whole chivalric canon of ridiculous books is one by one given over to the consecration of fire. The Critical. That's the EarthMotherBed of the whole enterprise. The Critical is its Hot Zone. The foundation upon which all its blooms spring forth: the swayback horses and the windmill giants and the clouts and the calamities and the great misfortune that madmen have sometimes of being taken for objects of humor. To read *Don Quixote* is to think about reading *Don Quixote*. *Don Quixote* was written on the face of a mirror.

Imagination. People talk about imagination and reality as if it was not the very way in which they went about talking that kept them from any kind of realization around these issues. It is not a matter, nor will it ever be a matter, of whether or not there is any such a thing as "distinction," but of whether or not there is anything anywhere at all except empty faces shining out of cold seas; anything anywhere at all but the interweaving woof and enmeshing warp of infinite tiny vibrant threads.

Existential/Phenomenological. One could call *Don Quixote* existential. One could call *Don Quixote* phenomenological. One could call it the imprudent narrative of an irresolute person and leave it at that. To Miguel de Cervantes, nothing but praise is due. But upon the question of his *Don Quixote*, this masterpiece of inhumanity, one is well within one's rights to equivocate. If one considers the body blows alone that our hero sustains (echoed and sometimes redoubled in those delivered to Sancho Panza, his brilliantly befuddled sidekick) if, as I say, one acknowledges only the literal enumeration of limbs and ribs broken, jaws smashed, pates and shoulders drubbed (and dismisses the terrifying blanket tossing that Sancho Panza took while his master looked on, the verbal abuses, the sleep deprivation, the starvation, and the unrelenting humiliations imposed upon them both by the sun-streaked hallucinatory landscape through which they – master and squire, the one on his swayback Rocinante, the other on his tireless donkey – caper) then the plain physical unlikelihood of survival under such conditions cannot but impel the sensitive reader toward an instinctive, perhaps blindly self-protective, insistence that "this cannot be the tale of a human being, this cannot be the tale of one of us." It would be just too unbearably sad. Oh, yes, this is either a masterpiece of inhumanity or else it is the flaming ash of the whole human prospect going up in a flash of prophecy.

Kafka's Version. In Kafka's version, *The Truth about Sancho Panza*, Don Quixote is simply the name of Sancho Panza's demon. "Sancho Panza succeeded in the course of years . . . in so diverting from himself his demon . . . that this demon thereupon set out, uninhibited, on the maddest exploits. [And] . . . Sancho Panza had of them . . . [an] edifying entertainment to the end of his days." Sancho Panza's "demon," in the context of this story, in connection with the stylish, almost theatrical levity with which Kafka's prose sometimes engaged what were seemingly the most personal, naked, and tragic issues of self-in-the-world, casts (in my humble opinion) a penetrating light upon what Kafka might have felt to be his own connection to his own authorship. To me, Kafka's version (which is *DQ* crystallized by a kind of alchemy) is still just "whistling in the graveyard," but I am not unsympathetic to the charm of its rendering. Merely in it probity, it is one of the most remarkable pieces of criticism in literary history.

Michel Foucault. Foucault writes that, "Don Quixote's adventures . . . mark the end of the old interplay between resemblance and signs and contain the beginning of the new relation." In other words Don Quixote constitutes a threshold. "His whole journey is a quest for similitudes: the slightest analogies are pressed into service as dormant signs that must be reawakened." Or, as the sages of the East have put it: it is we ourselves who must be reawakened. The truth about reason is this: that a Don Quixote who cannot be grasped must be invented.

The Editor's Garden. The only effective editing that can be done, in the case of every writing, is upon the soul of its author. A poem can be fixed, but then the next and the next and the next must also be fixed. In the end, it is better first to fix oneself and then to write the poems with perfect ease. The idea behind editing is to sharpen and focus what is already there, not to deconstruct and reconfigure as though what was never there to begin with was going somehow to return. That animating force underlying the level of ideation that shapes the creative – Dylan Thomas' "force that through the green fuse drives the flower" – is what is being sharpened and focused, that for the next poem it will be all the more at the ready. One always revises to write the next poem, one never revises simply for the sake of revision.

> A poet must push on   push on
> into uncharted territory
> even if the act is one of doubtful temperance.
> It is a terrible thing   a terrible thing
> to be a poet   or a thrush for that matter
> warbling away in the wilderness.
> I have never dreamed nor wished for
> anything but absolute honest admiration
> and I have never once expected
> to be praised for any poem I ever wrote.
> Nothing much can be said and
> of that nothing   nothing
> much worth saying.
> It is not my hope
> to rock in winds
> between dimensions
> thinking neither
> one thing nor another.

The Riddle of "Don Quixote." Michel Foucault writes that, "*Don Quixote* is the first modern work of literature, because in it we see the cruel reason of identities and differences make endless sport of signs and similitudes; because in it language breaks off its old kinship with things and enters into that lonely sovereignty from which it will reappear, in its separated state, only as literature." That "only!" If one could zero in on precisely the word by which Foucault rides roughshod over the whole world of intentionality, it would be that "only." That "only" is an indication to me that the intrepid Foucault actually believes he has stumbled on the solution to the riddle of *Don Quixote* by treating it as merely "a system of signs." But *Don Quixote* is much more than that. *Don Quixote* is a hunger that many of us have borne, and by which many of us bear the traces of having once been ravished.

Nietzsche, Please. Only Foucault would believe he could get away with the line: "This accounts, no doubt, for the confrontation of poetry and madness in modern Western culture." "Yes, Monsieur," one wishes at such times to volley back to Foucault, "but does it account for why I pick my nose?" Foucault can be so maddening in his insularity that all a critic can do in hopes of penetrating his stony fortress is to hurl taunts. Nietzsche was the genius of all time at this, of course. Foucault can be thankful, indeed, that I am not Nietzsche. No one, though, I expect, at this or at any other time, can be thankful in any way for news of my nose . . . but truth be said it is an organ of divination, my nose . . . and if no one but me may ever say so, I am lucky to have it.

Issues of Mortality. "Mortality should not be the subject of too much to scrutiny," one thinks safely to oneself. "Better that death should find us in its time than that we should appear to be reaching out to find death." Like most perplexing thoughts, this one began very simply. But, in another place and time too far back to reach? One sees perhaps the little wooden toy box and the little wooden soldiers, and one knows how the solitary child begins to believe in the world as something of God's but as something, too, of his own making.

The Dynamic-Generative. Poetry is the space into which the dynamic-generative conveys itself. Poetry is not itself generative and the generative that Poetry then does contain (after the dynamic-generative has conveyed itself into that Poetry) is not itself in what the Buddhists call a "First Principle" condition. Poetry is like the Garden. Who made the Garden?

Nevertheless it contains both Adam and Eve. And it is Adam alone, apparently, to whom we are indebted for Poetry. And it is out of that Poetry – that naming that Adam began – that we can fairly say the game began. What game? What game is that? Oh, only the game of trying to trick God into believing that we are capable of venerating his creation and still, alongside this capability, capable of doing all those other things we wish to do for our own glory.

A Testament. Poetry is an utterance of faith. It is a testament. A sacrament. It is a sanctuary. It is where beasts and birds come together and dwell in peace and where triptychs prowl on craggy mountain facades. Poetry is the place where faith comes to reside when it has, or can find, no other home.

Courtesy. In critical interpretation courtesy is the most important thing. A generous nature will critique generously and a miserly nature will critique by crossing over two bony fingers, but to critique is a part of the condition (existence?) and there is not one of us who is immune from the condition.

Two Mistakes. It is a mistake to think that the function of criticism is to bring together or distinguish polarities. Rather, criticism functions as the midnight motel attendant who carries his light down a dark corridor and shows how many rooms are available. It is also a mistake to consider that the function of criticism has anything to do with the correction of error. It is about interplays. How this part and that, otherwise disparate, can interplay in the realm of idea.

The Beat Quixote. For the Beats, Quixote was just another Zen Lunatic on a quest for enlightenment. But it really took some resolute self-delusion to maintain this stance. It was not Cervantes' Don Quixote, that is to say, but a shadow Don Quixote the Beats knew, created to be a reflection. The way, perhaps, Sartre made Flaubert an Existentialist.

One Perfect Poem. Who has written one perfect poem? Who? Name me someone who has written one perfect poem. Now, name me someone who has written more than one. Name me ten who have written two. Now all of you who have never in your lives written any but perfect poems, raise your hands.

Interpretation. It is a mistake to think that not everything can be interpreted. Everything can be interpreted so long as the condition of interpretation is clearly understood to be a subjective issuance. Now this may sound elementary to you and me, but there are some people who still do not understand it. All interpretation is psychological projection.

Don Quixote (As a Case-Study). A mad man, who believes himself a sane man, pretending to be a mad man.

Sancho Panza (As a Case Study). A dull man thrown upon a gyro.

Professor X. Professor X. tells me Cervantes' Lothario is no match for Shakespeare's. When I think "Lothario," I think neither Cervantes nor Shakespeare but *impresario.* I wonder if those *ario*s are bound etymologically or if it is just some fundamental similarity in their underlying connotation that I am conflating (someone surely to tell me absurdly). Cervantes' Camilla is a wet dream. Nowadays if an author has a wet dream it is called a nightmare. It is taken apart and picked over. But what if Eros and Psyche made their pact to co-exist, what then? A beautiful Camilla slowly ripening: the emerging feminine out of the romantic rot of patriarchal dominance, in any one of our lives? Alongside some damned Lothario, who, for his part in the pantomime, shows that anyone who has been tempted has already lost honor and that once honor is lost one might as well go all the way into depravity? If this is Cervantes' thought, it is a humbling and awful thought. If it is my own thought, then that is even worse.

Critique of a Feminist Tract. Talk about *gender* and *gendering*, I'd rather *engender*. There is a horrible price to pay for writing too many words even if it is a matter of filling so and so many pages.

DQ/Chapter 33. "Would you," writes Cervantes, "be doing the right thing if you conceived a desire to take this diamond and put it between a hammer and an anvil, so that by pure force you could find out if it was as hard and as fine as everyone said?" And of this book, *Don Quixote,* would one be doing the right thing to put *it* between a hammer and an anvil?

Performance and Representation. There is a way in which the performance is all and there is a way in which the representation is all, and there is a way in which the performance and the representation are nothing but projections through what might be called "a mind-space" and it is these projections that are everything, so that one finds in that mind-space, apparently one's own, the fertile *a priori* for which one had apparently been searching.

Mistake #1002. If I say something too personal that is one kind of mistake; if I say something too distant that is another. If there is anything to neglect in communication it is not the articulation of core courtesies; it is the articulation of core courtesies which allows our acceptance of the imprecise, the shifting, the ungrounded, the impossible complexity of all the rest of it.

Lines Written While Suspended on Wires Above an Abyss. The Phoenix has a little song he sings each time he goes to his death, but that does not mean the Phoenix's death is in any way different than our own. We might go with a song, as well. We might march right down into our green, green valleys singing our songs of death before we die and we will still be no more no less than the Phoenix who burns up again and again, and is reborn, on his passage through the sun. Deaths are all very much alike, the Phoenix sings. There is a moment of misfortune and calamity, but one grows used to that. Then there is the realization that one must now either choose forgetting or forgetting will simply occur. Then, in a moment, one is born through a stem like a lotus and delivered in perfection to the world.

The Camel's Song. The camel sings a song as he passes through the needle's eye. It goes something like this: "Hup! Hup! Ho! Hup! Hup! Ho!" There is a moment in this passage when it becomes a sexual event, and then somehow the camel twists through and is, if still a camel, now a camel passed through the needle's eye. The many and the profligate; the corrupt and the sectarian; the sages and the wild riders who wear their conquests gracefully on crests; and these emissaries, oh, these hapless emissaries, these delivery boys who make their livings taking messages to cemeteries.

The Book of Records. There is a book of records kept by a recording angel called the Celestial Record Book. In it, every moment and thought of our lives is registered on a plane of the ethereal in the form of a vibration. Think of it, every time you have masturbated, the most fully realized self-pleasuring you have ever given yourself, complete with its attendant thought patterns is limned there beyond anything like judgment. Like a blossom that fell from a blossoming tree in an orchard long ago.

Poets Laureate. Robert Frost, who wrote of the "slow, smoke-less burning of decay," was nevertheless never a candidate for the position of World Laureate of Poetry, which position I think all right-thinking critics can agree, at least since *The Duino Elegies* has been Rilke's to lose. Some might argue for Pablo Neruda and it is true that each of us has a blindness in the same proportion as he has a vision, but I just don't find that Neruda pierces reality deeply enough. He stays alongshore, like a heron, which is perfectly justifiable (any one of us might do the same for any number of enormous reasons) but then his profligacy (especially in the face of Rilke's parsimoniousness poem-making) makes me ask myself again: What is the value of one hundred poems, or one thousand, relative to the value of just one?

Male Poets. Poetry is a Cosmic Mother resource. Male poets who do not take advantage of this usually die of drink or other nervous disorders.

Guerilla Warfare. One does not engage the Muse in guerilla warfare. Wait, only what the Muse might say in a moment of inspiration matters, not what one can draw from her by sneaking up upon.

Some Lines. Some lines are better than others. Some books, too. And, some readers.

Golden Fruit. On the tree of gold, the golden fruit grows. But there can never be a golden seed.

Apples. Apples on the Tree of Knowledge? More like peaches and pears! More like plums and little berries. More like what I feel carnally to be the fruit of such a tree. Adam was never unknowing. It was always, from the moment of the creation, going to be only a question with Adam of what he would seek to understand. Adam was never innocent. Not for one moment.

The Devil. "How are your boundaries holding up?" he asks her with a devilish grin. "Terribly well, I'm afraid," she replies, lying as one does to the devil not so much to maintain one's virtue as to maintain one's self-respect.

Editor to Poet. Editor to Poet says: "Either poetry holds a charge or it does not hold a charge. Your poetry holds a charge. I would only be the mad electrician who strips away the insulation to make the lines more dangerous."

A Text of Criticism. To consider Cervantes' *Don Quixote* as anything but a text of criticism, a book of theories, a chancellery of howls and moans, a cauldron of souls half cooked over the fires of hell, a lovers lament from the unrequited Sancho Panza for his mad Master, a cry, from the realm of the Phoenix, for a new realm (for God's sake!) before the next miraculous rebirth, is to consider Cervantes' *Don Quixote* too shortly. To consider Cervantes' *Don Quixote* as a legend, though, is to take rather too long a view of it. To consider Cervantes' *Don Quixote* as a mirror and to leave it at that, seems the most likely do the issue justice over time. (Obviously, I am not the first to call a book a mirror. Lichtenberg famously wrote that "If an ape looks into a mirror, an apostle cannot possibly look out." Though I do believe that even an ape looking into *Don Quixote* might catch a glimpse of something uncanny.)

Everyman. Don Quixote is an Everyman. His follies are our follies. His foibles are our foibles. We, too, tilt at windmills, we too mistake trees for giants and wear toilet buckets on our heads from time to time. And who hasn't received a thousand and one blows from destiny and misfortune? He's just a guy, just a regular old Everyman, that Don Quixote, but what the hell can anyone make of that Sancho Panza? Now there's *el Diablo*, the Daemon Muse. (But, riding in on a donkey? Not in Jesus' posture, he's not! Crossing into his own personal Jerusalem, is he?) What the hell can anyone make of him? Just a crude depiction of the cruel feudal system and leave it at that?

Other Worlds

Suicide. Suicide is only for those who do not realize that they are already dead. There are no "other worlds." There is only the continuation of this world into the unknown. Would that transformation were as simple as disembodying oneself. Until the transformation that consumes the seed, there can be no real changes, only unimportant, formal distinctions.

Impossible Deeds. You who insist to me what can and cannot be done, do not insist but prove to me by undoing my "impossible deeds." The sky is hung upon a pearl like a blue cloak pegged upon the face of the deep.

Passion Worlds. The body, of course, is its own undoing, but let's be reasonable! The passion world, as yet unquaffed, for our thirst returns and not merely for its own concerns. "The Spring has need of us," as Rilke says, and to what malign winter do we consign ourselves, otherwise, everlastingly?

Immortality. "If it is not true," Chesterton wrote, "that a divine being fell, then one can only say that one of the animals went completely off its head." Even the continuum of immortality is suspect when it is broken down into its component parts for analysis. But who can say which of us is the madman and which of us the one who dwells within the wrong house?

The Soul. "To write well, lastingly well, immortally well . . . must one not cleave unto the muse?" wrote Pope. "Such a task scarce leaves a man time to be a good neighbor . . . much less to save his soul." The soul! That bright little bundle. Mustn't it be ever reconsidered in the light of its domicile? Sometimes it is more important for the soul to be lost than it is for the soul to be saved. One must learn the value of everything before a life course can be truly set.

Heaven's Gate. In terms of the creative, knowledge is detrimental, belief imperative. Beauty becomes the more inscrutable, the more of itself it reveals. Heaven's gate upon heaven swings open. Heaven upon heaven is laid.

Compromise. The soul of communication is compromise. If I wish my art to communicate, I will myself to accept compromise. If those compromises seem to undermine the spirit of whatever artistic endeavor I am pursuing, then I do not abandon compromise, I abandon the endeavor.

Not Good Enough. The idea that what you have created is not "good enough" is simply preposterous – and maddening! How is the quality of what you have created – and let's not even go into the subjectivity of that determination – even relevant? The created is created for the sake of the creation, not for the sake of the evaluation. The creative is of the creative. The evaluative is of the evaluative. I do not say of my lover, "Yes, but what use would she be parsing a complex mathematical equation?" Oh, judgment, hold your gavel – for once – in suspense!

The Life Flowing. The life flowing into the writing and out again must be as the sleeping mind is to the mind awake: both a resource and a thing in and of itself.

Genuine Efforts. The genuine efforts of human beings to communicate with one another: that is what literature is composed of. We say the novel is dead? It is not that the novel is dead, but that we ourselves have moved on into the next world.

Eros. To know God is to dare to fall. Faith is a leap in one's own face. "Mere human honesty," wrote Kierkegaard. Eros! Where is there more proof? We are bound to make mistakes. "Erotic love is self-love," wrote Kierkegaard. "Friendship is self-love." Well, then, to arms! If a battle it must be, then let it be a battle using only what weapons God gave us. Naked I came. Naked I will make my way. And you, oh, my fellow warrior, on what bow are you strung? Faith, my dear, faith! I have heard the music of our wedding day.

The Novel. The novel is a bully that has held sway over writers for too long. It is artful enough to deliver one compelling sentence. Not to mention sufficiently indubitable.

Religion. One need not speak of one's belief in order to be "religious." In fact, one ought not. The God of literature is the completion of the text. Zealotry is always profligate.

The Poet's Heart. "The sea tumbling in harness," wrote Dylan Thomas. Could that not be the poet's heart in a moment of passion? Oh, but the solitude of the creative act is unassailable. Without fire we could not be sure what finally is here just to be consumed and what is pretty much here for the duration.

Your Symbols. Your symbols are not my symbols but symbols are all we have and no symbol is enchanted but meaning is.

Unforgettable. "Unforgettable" is an adjective that one uses with regard to certain people, places, or incidents on the way to "forgotten."

The Absurd. "It is," as Cardinal Newman observed, "as absurd to argue persons, as to torture them, into believing." But, get this! The dead live. Those who do not recognize the absurd are doomed to propound it.

Some Writers. Some writers appear to believe that the dullness of their writing is a virtue. That it reflects well upon the steadiness of their character. When in fact it is merely the humiliating result of the steadiness of their character.

Teacher. I consider myself a teacher. But let no one presume from that definition a condition of morality. My field is aesthetics. Who does not prefer the human Jesus to the absent perfection of The Heavenly Father? Or what ought an artist to be born for if not his flaws?

Genius. Genius is best which absents itself from the materialization. Perfection should always seem in the design, not in the origination.

Men and Women. "To long for the transcendent when you are in your wife's arms," writes Bonhoeffer, "is, to put it mildly, a lack of taste. If he pleases to grant us some overwhelming earthly bliss, we ought not to try to be more religious than God himself." Philosophies are how? Men are whom? Women are what? Hmm . . . but, in fact, there is neither truth, nor gender. There are only distinctions, momentarily appropriate.

The Smoke of Fire. The function of art is to invigorate. In this way it is much like love and inspires, on the part of the rationalists, a similar distrust. "Talent without genius isn't much," wrote Valery, "but genius without talent isn't anything at all." Indeed, sir? But do not all things originate in the divine? When I am cut, do I not bleed? Art is merely the instinct of form to propagate itself in a manner consistent to its own continuity. Like life, it is neither the mirror of fire, nor the smoke of fire, but the fire itself.

The Page. The page is always blank to begin with. That is the virtue of it. "My ideas are my whores," wrote Diderot. So, too, will the page yield to any master. To write is no achievement at all, only to write well.

My Teachers. It would be capricious of me not to thank my teachers. But where they might be now, I have no way of knowing. The spirit is invested with beings who seem in retrospect all to have been oneself.

The Writer. Remember, first of all, that the writer must be amusing himself. Then, how telling of the personality of the writer the writing becomes.

II

More About Art. Lately I came across the phrase, "The artist is always more important than the art," in one of those New Age texts, and I could scarcely contain my indignation. Really! Some artists will do anything to justify a limping prose style. The artist who tells you that his life is his most "sublime" creation is lacking either in dignity or in capacity. Anyone can muster an army. Art is always, and only, in the conquest of self.

Words. There are no words. There are only angels of light and of darkness.

Biographical Criticism. The history of biographical criticism is a history of mistaking the recipient of the message for the messenger.

The Life of an Artist. To analyze the life of an artist through his work is sort of like analyzing personality through dream interpretation. One can find correlations, but there is always the possibility that a dream is not a mirror, but another world entirely.

Yes to Draw Down No. Art is neither one thing nor another. Neither spirit, nor matter – necessarily. It is simply the rendering of what is at that moment charged with verisimilitude. You and I, for instance, in the simple act of surrendering. Yes to draw down No upon her bosom – and murder him!

My Opinions. At least my opinions are my own, and not the result of some farcical process of "painstaking research." I came upon them idly, and subsequent personal experience has either emboldened or negated my initial sense of their piquancy. What ought a real scholar to do, except finger "the-devil-may-care" on accordion, when all about him are those who would confine all orchestration to those musics which can be played by an ensemble made up entirely of fine tooth combs and paper clips. Agree or disagree. The real question is whether or not one can dance to it.

Socrates. Every case is individual. Thus, one does not conclude from the case of Socrates and his daemon that the voices in so-and-so's head are not merely schizophrenia. Each person's method ought to be entirely his or her own affair. However, if the product of that method is set before us, that we may judge. The work of a madman, and what "looks like the work of a madman," may be two different things. As might madness itself.

Humility. His simplicities are – of course – complexities artfully disguised, whereas my simplicities are merely simplicities. It's all in the eye of the beholder, we know, but does reticence count for nothing these days unless it is pointing itself out?

Academia. It is rather a jungle where one must not devour without seeming first to pause.

Contradiction. Contradiction is a walkover. After all, who in history has ever been proved entirely right? The measure of genius is in the creation of alternatives. It is less important to oppose the current paradigm than it is to disregard it.

The Soul of Our Age. I am absolutely convinced that there is nothing to be either gained or lost by any of our activities. This sounds like an existential politic, I'll admit, but I think it does not preclude the possibility of even Christian redemption. It just puts us in the position of being post-ethical in our mores, which just about catches us up with the soul of the age.

Difficult. It is difficult, especially when one really is a poet, not to fatally imagine oneself a poet, and thence destroy any immediate chance one has of actually writing poetry.

Artist and Visionary. The distinction between artist and visionary is not entirely irrelevant. Though it need not necessitate two separate individuals, it often does (and in many more cases it ought). Visionaries have a tendency to fall under the spell of their own visions. This makes them often not the best communicators. "It is!" they cry, like an arrow to the deep. Whereas an artist might paint his starry sky, take a deep breath, and step back quietly into his waiting.

Critical Ideas. You think critical ideas are important. I think critical ideas are important only insofar as they are conducted creatively. An argument between any two people is only as important as the ideas being argued: that is, were the ideas abstracted from their personal context and made wholly theoretical. Most of argument is so wholly futile that it demeans not only the participants, but the very idea of Logic – upon which it is ostensibly founded. All logic is paradoxical at root and at zenith, because it depends upon the airtight reasoning faculties of its disseminator (at one end) and upon the presumption of a condition called "finality" at the other. We can reason only to the limits of our understanding, and if we believe that the limits of our understanding are commensurate to the limits of understanding, well then . . .

Energy. Energy – finally – into the expansion of ego-as-Self, or into the expansion of self-as-Self. That is, into the personal, or into the universal aspect of Being. History shows the futility of the former, while of the latter, nothing whatever – good or ill – may be stated with any confidence at all.

III

Love. A he and a she . . . . Well, let us not say a man and a woman, but one who loves already and one who would willingly be made to love. There is a time, and if that time passes and love has not found its way into both hearts . . . . A tree overhangs a waterfall. A willow tree of long hanging branches. From a distance, by the arrangement of the pair, it may appear that many tears pour out of the trees. As many as might be held back in the course of a loveless life. A he and a she . . . . But, well, let us not say a man and a woman.

Matchmaker. I have always had a talent for literary matchmaking. For getting the right person together with just the right piece of prose. It is not everyone who gets sufficient nourishment feeding at the trough of German Romanticism, or who finds in the rarefied top drawer of British wit, that exact right jewel with which to adorn himself. But everyone has, somewhere, some few words which, if they are not absolutely necessary to their formal well-being, are imperative to their soul's delight.

Greatness. There are two directions toward which any of us can aspire: the greatness of the personality, or the greatness of the humanity. And these two directions are mutually exclusive. The former depends upon amplification. The latter upon submission.

Herr Professor. Your writing is certainly unimpeded by any sense of personal style. Perhaps that is because you believe your ideas to be so entirely original that they can stand on their own merits? Alas, dear sir, you are just one of a million shadows cast by a great light.

P.S. You think my criteria too rigorous? Perhaps that is because the ideas I propound are so elementary. A little more soul, dear sir, and a little less disquisition upon the moral imperative. It is not, after all, as if the categorical preceded the creative.

Art. Art is the constraint that one imposes upon the delirium of the canvas. There is nothing "blank" about it, except inasmuch as it is in one's own mind. But, if everything is possible, what, then, is creditable? Thereupon arises the question of aesthetics. (And the necessity for an aesthetic? One must suppose so. However, between the elation of genius and the gravity of genius, there is nothing to choose.)

Experience. It has been my experience that those who imagine themselves "doomed," are of fundamentally more romantic a temperament than those who consider themselves "religious." Quite the opposite of what is commonly held to be the case.

Man. The philosopher chooses man, "the multitude," the priest chooses man, "the totality."

Bodies. Between any two pressed bodies together there remains a thin sheet of light through which the sense of touch is transported.

On the Fear of Irony. When one is caught up in the romance of seeking, or when one seeks without faith, there is some danger of becoming ironic. Do not avoid it! A snail upon the roof / Ah, but nowhere a home.

The Phenomenological World. Is it artistry enough merely to have the vision? Or ought not an artist to be (in equal part, at least) a "facilitator?" One can represent the phenomenological world as esoteric, merely by rendering (or attempting to render) in parts its entirety, or one can render a single phenomenon and thereby encompass that entirety in a part.

Contemporary Poetics. People who can't write are touted as poets? What next? People who can't think will be touted as visionaries? As if to speak clearly implied some hapless lack of sophistication. What is that you say? "The presence is implied by the absence?" By that logic what could not be proven to be the case? Truth does not exist, therefore trust only the liar? When the absurd becomes the standard by which logic is adjudged – well, then, my legions, pull off your masks! The devil has won over the church.

Doubt. The one who suffers his doubt will find more allies in this world than the one who reveals his hope. Nevertheless, I would not choose to become a philosopher, even if it left me no alternative but the priesthood.

Mistakes. I kept making the same mistake over and over – and the mistake I kept making was in somehow thinking that poetry was something separate from myself.

Hero. It is surely not the voice that comes out of the singer, but the voice that comes through the singer, just slightly misshaped by the passage that I prefer to hear, oh.

Deus Ex Nihilis! Am I bitter? Of course! Idiot theorists have taken over the one field in which I am competent to practice. The field of higher education. The lip service of cretins counts more to the fire than a basket of sparks, apparently. But, to give credit where credit is due, they are at least well-intentioned, whereas I would have dismantled the whole thing block by block, starting with the thoughts of the so-called masterworks and going down to the toenails of those who have written the latest progressive handbooks. What would I have left standing had they let me in? Only you, my friend, and I – and the unquenchable force by which the whole institution would have resurrected itself in an as yet unknown and entirely unknowable form.

Not to Mention. Has anyone else called the Post-Modernist movement "neo-classical"? With its fantastically heightened sense of the primacy of form, what else could it be? Rebellion is merely the manner of its fascination.

You Scholars. You scholars who feign self-knowledge by modeling self-deprecation, when do you ever rest from your irony?

A Calling. I do it for many reasons. Not the least because it gives me pleasure. Who is to say what makes a priest. But a certain amount of hedonism, certainly.

Concluding Sermon. Art ought not to be water soluble. When I hear of a work that it is "disturbing," or "profoundly important," I know in an instant that time will wash it away. So what? Time will wash everything away? Is that what I hear you say? Ah, my friend, not everything. Not you and I. Therefore, let us not dance with questions that will answer themselves, hoping to steal away from life its mystery by presuming upon its meaning, or its meaning by presuming upon its mystery. In fact, my friend, let us pray to remain unknowing, so that we may continue to live and die. What better fate could we ask from our maker? And for our making, what better fate? May the art of our children's children be our Father's art! He who shrouded in the finite all but our faith.

My Religion

Bridge or a Wall. If you write in order to develop a relationship with your fellow human beings and your writing becomes the sole constitution of that relationship then is your writing a bridge or a wall?

That Need. If we are writing in order to displace a need – and few, it might be argued, are not – then how can we ever hope to come to terms with that need? That is to say: the writing might make terms, but that is like putting the splint on the shadow of the broken leg.

Writing Itself. Not the morality or ethicality of any particular kind of writing, but the morality or ethicality of the act of writing itself. A vainer – in both senses of the word – pursuit there never was. Even the great Nietzsche was ashamed on that account.

The Blessing from the Curse. To what ought language be applied, if the measure of its virtue is in how it ameliorates? And what then, if the answer is, "to itself only," is the virtue of language? Shall we say: that it produces more and better language? Separate who is able, in language's case, the blessing from the curse.

Language. Language has the power to charm, but only you and I have the power to dispassionately observe. Language must always fall on one side or the other of every issue. This is its failing. Basho said, "The problem with language is that it is always either too subjective or too objective." I can't top that, although I filtered his phrase somewhat to suit my own semiotics. Rather than "language," Basho used the term, "poetry."

Poetasters. For every gift, there is a recipient. That is the wretched assertion of every poetaster.

Magician. The magician will get bored of his magic tricks long before the audience does, but it is the magician's boredom that will eventually tell on the reception of the tricks. Laughter is the actualization of the material principle of transcendence. The comic and the profound, and oh, yes, the erotic, are the actual Holy Trinity.

First Note on the Academics. Realize that many academics are savvy, in the way of small time politicians, or petty lawyers. They never get caught telling the truth, and lie only to flatter.

One Terrible Law. There is only one terrible law in all of Karma: whatever you mock you will eventually become. That, my friends, is why I mock the rich and the beautiful.

First Note on Identity. Identity, at least in the abstract, is entirely conditional – evolving as a means of address. That is to say, it is adaptive and therefore transitory. So that when any one of us settles into a self of fixed materiality, he or she is attempting to make conduct more powerful than process. A ridiculous vanity, the conviction of which leads to dogmatism, which leads to every sort of conflict. Identity is a means of encountering the world, not a medium through which to control it. This is so simple that thousands of years of history have not made it any easier to understand. The world is so much more powerful than we are – driven by forces so much more cosmic and fundamental – that to stand fast before their onrush is a form of suicide. And, at the level of our mere humanity, a bad bit of modeling to pass along to our progeny.

Pre-verbal. The root of every conviction is pre-verbal. The idea that language represents is not the embodiment of that idea, but a shadow which falls from that idea.

First Note on Literature. Literature is predominately representational – that is to say, a compromise toward communication through the shadow medium of language. This compromise necessarily precludes the communication of that pre-verbal origin. It is not the question, however, of the sincerity of literature that we are pursuing, but of the condition of its generation. Literature, it has been said, is a lie that leads us to the truth. Well, not exactly. Literature is a lie that unlike other lies can be grasped and dissected. ("Deconstructed," in the current argot.) Literature is a more material and therefore less slippery lie than most. That materiality is its virtue. Language is like a criminal whose guilty conscience forces him to leave clues at the scene of the crime.

Sentimentality. Literature prospers solely by the sentimentality of the reader. This is not to say that sentimentality is a sick condition, just that it is a condition of innocence. Since one cannot be innocent beyond one's awareness of that state – since innocence will transition into experience – what, ultimately, shall we ask of literature? That is to say, since literature cannot be a guide to the experienced reader in terms of delivering moral or ethical determinations, what shall we ask of it? One wants to reply: "Pleasure," but – Oh, Socrates! – what pleasure is it, if not of deep moral or ethical resonance, that is not a lesser in the range of human possibilities? One might console oneself that language – at least ideally – like John the Baptist, knows itself to be at hand only to prepare a place for the greater thing that comes after. The prophecies, that is to say, are not nothing. In fact, they are a wondrous something. Save but in relation to The Presence Itself.

First Addendum. Literature comes to prepare a place, to make ready. (Although the miracle of His Presence – if it really is His Presence – shouldn't that overwhelm any objections, with or without preparation? I mean when the Gods come from the sky and stand before us all aflame, will any really say, "I see them, but only because I was made ready to see them?" Not much of our definition of the God-condition would seem to pertain, if that was the case.)

Embodiment. Embodiment, one might say, is literature in its mystic condition. Representation, one might say, is literature in its dialectical condition. Embodiment is an issue of grace. Representation, an issue of will. The product of will is more will. The product of grace is more grace. Will can be twisted. Grace cannot even be grasped.

Mockery. We mock one another, cheerfully, out of our strengths. Why is it that we do not so assertively bow down before one another out of our weaknesses?

My Religion. My religion is a sort of surreal existential mysticism in which the resurrected Christ embodied as a tiger lays plastic flowers on the grave of Jean-Paul Sartre. It is a performance as distinct from the soul as the shadow that falls from a harlequin in a music hall, and as undying in its association.

Zealotry. I have only two real interests: the nature of the creative impulse, and one other that I don't know how to speak of. Blake's "enthusiasm for art!" Would we say Saint Francis' "enthusiasm for Jesus?" But to call it zealotry is somehow to damn it faintly, as if it were based on mania – that daughter of neurosis. True artists are apostles. True art is not different from – indeed is identical to – religious vision.

Reverences. Poetry reverences, or ought to reverence, communication. Mysticism reverences, and must reverence, realization. There are, of course mystic-poets, but poet-mystics are almost inevitably deluded scholars (unconsciously?) recapitulating arcane traditions. Earnest scholarship is a useful prerequisite to mystic attainment, but best if it were accomplished, and forgotten, in a previous lifetime.

Academic Theorists. Academic theorists are predominately aristocratic and not democratic in their sympathies. They are happy enough to communicate solely with one another. And surely the heaven toward which they aspire will not include those gentle, confused souls whom the theorists say to encompass with their knowing. (I mean, for the sake of both factions.) Poets have some justification for writing critical theory. I mean, poets of genius. Not that it aids them in understanding themselves, but that it might hinder posterity a little from arriving at some of its more egregious misinterpretations. Nothing, however, can protect the poet of genius from the Desperate Doctoral Thesis. Not even the fundamental absurdity − vanity? malevolence? − of the undertaking.

The Holy Bible. Perhaps The Holy Bible was written in "the final days" of its world. A memorial, of sorts, as opposed to a visionary work. The only inspired aspect of it being that revolutionary style which makes it such a compelling read. Would it really be so strange to live in a world for which a Bible had not yet been written? Or, rather, say we have no need of prophecy in this age, having at hand so much of history for reference.

On Baudelaire's "The Painter of Modern Life." I had found these essays distasteful, the opinions rudely expressed, until it occurred to me that the slanted prose was a necessary function of the position. Baudelaire was "the council for the defense," in the never-ending "case against art." Considering the prosecution's historical "restraint," it is no wonder he fortified himself with some weaponry. What was he to do with his wit? Cast it aside? It was more than enough already to have made it so subtle. When have the prosecution ever entered swinging less than a bludgeon or a cudgel? What use a naked man to come striding across the courtroom floor – if it please the jury! – when his righteousness has already been deemed "of no account."

Revolutionary Methodologies. Revolutionary methodologies accomplish nothing. A superficial rearrangement of the dominant paradigm, whereby the rich and the poor exchange places. Injustice is overturned, but oppression remains. Ah, you might respond, but did anyone say we were trying to create Paradise? Well . . . yes! However wrong-headedly a Christ figure might have arisen in the midst of such proceedings, I do believe something of the sort was suggested in the midst of those first secret meetings. I'll make you a deal, though: I won't niggle over motivations, if you don't presume it was the superiority of your logos that made you victorious. The whole world's in disrepair. It don't take a flaming sword to slice through a pat of butter. Your flesh, or mine, my dear one.

Theory. Theory is the ghost that rises from the corpse upon the dissecting table.

The Function of Beauty. The romantic sense of the "function" of beauty is that it elevates humanity. That it gives one a glimpse of the higher world. Such a notion carries down, of course, from Plato, for whom beauty is the shadow of the divine. But what if one were to look at it in another sense: the sense in which there are no shadows, that nothing is representative of anything else. That the "function" of beauty is simply to sustain beauty. Just as the function of the grotesque is simply to sustain the grotesque. There is no question that if the divine exists at all, it does not exist as only one end of a spectrum. The divine is a spectrum, of which, for instance, one aspect is the grotesque, another the invidious, another the mediocre.

Note to a Fellow Theorist. True! Dissolution completes formulation. If, that is, created objects move along a straight line from their point of conception. Rather, though, I believe that objects (artistic creations, if you will!) are unendingly cyclical events which pre-exist themselves in the realm of possibility. That point of stasis at which, under the artist's hand, the object is made manifest to the senses, is merely a reflection of the aesthetic principles of that particular artist. From whence is the idea of chaos derived, if not from its relationship to order? Or what is darkness, if not the irresolution of light? In fact, sir, what does not contain its opposite? You and I? It would be daft to deny our communion!

Cut-Ups. My argument with the technique of "cut-ups" derives from the fact that it requires no extraordinary sensibility to accomplish. One needs only a moderately well-developed ability to make associations. I like to believe that art is that which is done by artists. Not merely "play," but "play" in tandem with a highly developed faculty of discrimination. True enough, the arts may thence become the realm of the effete, but better that than it become merely another "opiate of the masses." We already have religion drawn from a tap, let us not now sell colored water as wine.

Notes to Certain Graduate Students. You'd think we could learn how to get along. I mean, of course, the unwashed realists, and those "literalists of the imagination" who have just recently stepped down from the clouds. But since when did plagiarism become a "literary technique"? If someone writes an essay, and you agree with everything it says, "right down to the very marrow of your being," does that give you the right to sign your name to it and sell it as your own? A poem is not a petition, it is a sacred event. However, I suppose if you do not even believe in the sacred there will be no question of whether or not you would sell "the holy bones," so long as you can find someone stupid enough to believe they can really be bought and paid for. The spirit is not in the relic, but in the mystery attached to its emanation.

Three Language Poets. Language Poet X complains that I am trying to promote "the bourgeois epiphany." "What a great line," I reply. "Why can't you write more lines like that? Phrasings that a lay-poet like myself can understand?" Language Poet X receives this communication not as a compliment to her sensibility but as an insult to her poetry. Language Poet Y does not realize that she has entered the empire in the period of its decay. It will be funny when Language Poet memoirs begin to appear, and then when the memoirs begin to overshadow the work itself, and then when – as with the poetry of the Dadaists and the Surrealists – only a few poems of the epoch remain for the edification – and as a jumping off point – for future generations. July 1st, 2005. As of today, it is as laughable to pursue a Language Poet ethos as it would be to pursue an ethos Aristotelian. Meanwhile Language Poet Z writes on un inter upt ed ly.

Professor X. Professor X would like to know if I consider myself a poet or a prose writer. "I consider myself a word stylist," I reply. "A sort of prestidigitator of phonemes. A performance artist working on the page. A mimic. A critic." I tell him everything but the truth, which is that I believe I am an intermediary between the invisible and the visible worlds. Professor Y simply smiles paternally, accepts the honest – if charged up account – of my current creative project at face value. I get the distinct impression that he finds me tremendously interesting. Even if this is simply the ingrown politic of a born department head, it is still damn reassuring. The cruel and the kind, dear friends, the cruel and the kind. There is no other division, there are no other deeds.

Notes from a Reading. I get the feeling with B. that he thinks he sees something in me more than he expected and it interests him. I am hardly ever a mystery to anyone. I have made that my policy. It is also the consequence of my autobiographical style. But, it is a bit seductive to be cast into that role and I am inclined simply as a matter of strategy – if this is the way I am to be viewed – to allow myself to be viewed this way. Certainly I have had no success with stripping myself down to the bone at the first nod of interest. I mean, no professional success. For artistic success, there is no other means but to immediately and thoroughly divest oneself of any obfuscation. I am not sure quite what to make of Q. It is possible that other than his poetic gift he is extremely dense. Many gifted artists are extremely dense. Some of them, if you can believe it, have not even any insight into themselves. L. I don't trust at all. He is an entirely social creature. On the other hand, he would make a great protector. That is, if he could see any reason to render me that service. Meaning, if he could conceive of some useful reciprocation I might ultimately provide. When I say he is "entirely social," I mean that his relationship to the world is utterly strategic. Utterly based in a predilection for social power. I want power, too, of course, everyone does. But unlike someone like L., I am not prepared to pursue it at any cost. Z. reminds me of my ex-wife. Same body type. Same high intelligence. Same streak of willful independence that is doubtless a masquerade that disguises a fundamentally subservient nature. Had I understood this earlier about my ex-wife, I could doubtless have created a sexual dynamic that would have been satisfying for us both. It is for this, no doubt, slightly sinister reason that I sometimes look at Z. and imagine myself marrying her.

The Avant-Garde. The standards of the avant-garde are so high that there is no possible application. Even the avant-gardes themselves realize the impossibility of achieving their aesthetic. This is why they are so bitter. The real avant-garde is the expansion of the possible beyond the prior definition of its limits, not merely the expansion of the prior definition of the limits. It is substance that informs evolution.

A Defense of My Absurdist Nature. My genius is characterized by its flaws, in deference to the mediocrity from which it arises. In thought, one must not be afraid of the trivial. "The high rests on the low," as Lao-Tzu put it.

Résumé. Clown, scientist and poet. Now there is a resume one could live with. And rather than "writer," anything, even "whore" would be preferable.

Nabokov. Nabokov said that "reality" was the only word in the English language that should always be surrounded by quotation marks. Not "reality," but "dream."

II

The Moment of Settling. Immediate inspiration! For which the notebook format is ideal. But first, one must be a bona fide "thinker." That is, one for whom the forward progress of thought is constant, even at the moment of settling it into a form. Reason is the serpent that strains against its own skin. Knowledge is only detrimental to those who have not yet learned to release it once it has been grasped. Eve was cast out of Eden, not for eating the apple, but for failing, before she did so, to befriend the serpent (her shadow self, really, attempting to teach her something about the true nature of thought). The fall, then, was inevitable, but not necessarily the exile.

Paradise. It is okay for me to remain in paradise, even though I know I am estranged from my maker. After all, nothing is elsewhere than here more easily resolved. That is, no cell lends itself more readily to contemplation than does every garden.

The Question. The question, it seems to me, is did Adam have competent legal counseling, and if, as it seems, he did not, are we now at too late a date to declare a mistrial? Certainly we ought not to be, considering the ramifications of the decision.

The Initial Impulse. The initial impulse to write can be most anything, but the continuing impulse can only be neurotic, considering what the author must learn about himself and about the world (its values and evaluations), even if he is successful. Or, perhaps, especially if he is successful.

Types. I do not understand why we, as individuals, cannot realize that we are merely predictable "types" occupying historical "positions," with regard, say to our sense of moral conduct, or our ideas about reasoning. Always, there will be someone arguing on the side of a logic derived entirely from sense data and someone arguing on the side of intuition. Can we not just look at one another and wink, even while we construct our airless dialectical positions in one another's despite? Surely it is all more comic than it is serious.

One Side. The logical on one side, the intuitive on the other. Or, is it the intuitive on one side, the logical on the other. No matter, just so long as there is an opposition against which to define ourselves. Where would we be without the "other?" Or, rather, who? But, this is an identity?

The Mystic. When the mystic stares into the eternal, he becomes the eternal. This is neither an act of will, nor a voyage of self-discovery. It is an acknowledgment of the inwardness of outwardness, which is to say it is an acknowledgment of the fact that no division exists.

Authorship. Authorship is an occult property. Therein lies its danger to the one who pursues it for any sake other than the common weal.

Ideas. Ideas are inherently grammatical and their power is purely that of their construction. That is to say: form contains (but not necessarily to say: idea dissipates). One idea is as good as the next, so long as it really is an idea, and not just a vapor masquerading as an embodiment. The flowers of method so quickly become the flowers of madness.

Nietzsche and Kierkegaard. Whereas Nietzsche thundered his philosophies as if from a pulpit, Kierkegaard performed his as if for a puppet theater. That is to say, Kierkegaard's instincts were dramatic and communal (deriving in spirit from the parables of Jesus), whereas Nietzsche's instincts were philological and didactic (deriving in spirit from the dialogues of Socrates).

An Author Like S.K. An author like SK (Soren Kierkegaard) can be revered (or despised) in a way that I will never be revered (or despised) because SK was willing to risk the appearance of foolishness, whereas I protect myself at all times behind a veil of irony. Not to mention the fact that his works are prodigious, whereas mine are effete. (A distinction I think we can safely attribute to the variance in our levels of personal vanity, not to mention our conceptions of who, ultimately, are the constituents of our readership.)

Details. We know a lot about the details of SK's life, and his output attests to the quality of his discipline, but about what it was like to be SK at the time in which his pen dipped, trembling, into the inkwell, we can know nothing. The mystery of authorship is not in the conduct of the life, but in the measure of the author's presence or absence from the pages to which he must ultimately sign his name. It was this consideration, I think, as much as any merely dialectical augmentation to the proceedings that induced SK to the use of metaphoric pseudonyms – Constantine Costantius, Johannes de Silentio – in his early aesthetic work. And by the same token, the fact that SK dispenses with pseudonymous self-assignation in his later "religious" works and signed his own, given name, was not necessarily because he had become there so truly, fully himself, but perhaps because there he had no personal identity at all. Authorship is a struggle between the personal and the profound.

Innocence. I'll never again be innocent, but I can still experience innocence through others, can I not? That is what the profession of teaching is all about, and the pastime of seduction.

III

Point of Clarity. The Holy Bible does not prove the existence of Jesus, any more than a biography of Winston Churchill proves the existence of Winston Churchill. The only thing the Bible or any other document, in its isolation, proves is its own existence. The only thing that can be said, positively, for the Bible as an historical document is that it does not refute the existence of Jesus. Which at least gives the possibility a running start.

Some Issues. The body made word and word made bread: this is the transmutation. One can hardly imagine Jesus as the priest at a Catholic mass. Ritual that does not feed the spirit, whatever its intention, is desecration. Word is either bread or stone. Or, as they say in the new gospel: living or dead. Religion is art. That is, religion is not an organization of principles to be maintained at any cost, but a living entity, as the root of its rising – inspiration – would indicate.

Zen Blake. I admit it, things can get pretty crackpot when you are trying to defend the religious impulse against the priests. This accounts for the Zen heritage in Buddhism on one hand and for a poet like William Blake on the other.

Without which, and whom, I might add, this world might have long since become a cold, dark cloister.

Saint Jennifer. "I go braless in a white T-shirt every time it rains," she says, "because there are men out there who have nothing at all."

Genius Blake. In the notebooks, Blake says of Haley that Haley is "the friend of my body, but the enemy of my spirit," and implores him to "do be my enemy for friendship's sake." Do you see where this is going? The artist must nurture his genius as a mother nurtures her child. Perhaps the artist, the mother, grows thin and wan, while the genius, the child, grows plump and jolly. Shall the artist, the mother, be protected from this parasite? As if! A willful misreading to the effect that the preceding reveals a burgeoning martyr complex is certainly possible. Consciousness IS the crown of thorns. There is no more apt metaphor than that. The martyrdom of the saints, though, is to the martyrdom of the poets, approximately what a red hot impalement is to a cream pie pummeling.

To Oppose God. Imagine a person whose destiny it was to oppose God. To which end he had been granted an arsenal of superhuman weapons. Including the gift of insight (shallow, perhaps, but very definitely genuine) into the mind of God. Now, imagine if he then adduced that these weapons of opposition were even from God, who wanted to die. What then?

Kindness. Would we be kinder to one another, I wonder, if we thought that our kindness was the only thing keeping that other person alive?

Conscience. Everything I write is completely personal, as well as utterly disengaged. The issues of form, for me, always supersede the specificities of content. I draw entirely from my own life because I do not believe it is polite to speculate upon the inner world of anyone but myself. One would have to be both clairvoyant and magnanimous to do otherwise with anything like a clear conscience.

My Poetry. I am not a poet, but a comedian. My poetry lives and dies by how it amuses. Insight passes into commonplace and then platitude. Only laughter is eternal – the laughter of the Gods.

Sören Kierkegaard. I must take myself seriously, but without seeming to require that others do so as well. This predicament is the same as had the young SK, if I may say so, and is a spiritual, rather than a merely stylistic concern.

SK. Sometimes I think that all through my works should be interpolated the initials SK, so if my reader derives nothing else from it, he will be reminded, at least, of the existence of that great philosopher from whose writings I have accrued such personal bounty in the realm of spirit, and without whose example of magnanimity to the self, I would surely have become even more vainglorious and megalomaniac. "All crises are crises of faith," wrote poor SK. My fling with existentialism is my attestation to that!

Existentialist Notebooks

Authenticity. The controlled semblance, or appearance, of authenticity, in manner, in intonation, is enough to persuade me instantly of its (in fact) absence in deep actuality. Which is why I prefer the vestige of irony, even in my championing angels.

A Religious Tenet. A religious tenet, like a governmental statute, that makes independent thought a crime, is one step away from dictating what we ought and ought not to dream.

Smart Women. Smart women converse about how easily manipulated are men by this or that transparent wile to which they would be loathe to stoop. As if our desires were frauds that we were attempting to have perpetrated upon ourselves. A simple case, these conversations, of the women mistaking our objective, which is an end that so outweighs for us the means by which we might attempt its achievement as to render those means immaterial. All that we are we achieve by design, in any event, ladies. It is ultimately the condition of Being to which we subscribe in those cases. Not some mere aesthetic fallacy.

Tempered Steel. Anti-intellectualism, in our time, is supposed to be the intellectuality par excellence, but all it is, really, is irony that cannot sting pretending to be irony that will not sting. If you keep a dull blade sheathed, who can prove that it is not tempered steel?

Government. Government is a system of morality developed by philosophers and refined by mercenaries. Who says that we cannot rule ourselves? Well, yes, history, but why should she, rather than prophecy, have the last word?

Posterity. I have clearly begun writing to posterity, which is not, I pray, an indication of my hopelessness but rather of its (hopelessness') complete material conversion. I can hardly understand what I am saying, myself, at times. I can, however, feel the glimmer of future understanding, glowing within these words.

Nietzsche. "The posthumous one," wrote Nietzsche. A funny guy. An aristocrat upon the throne of his prospects. It is not surprising that he died mad, amidst the ghosts of his kingdom. I'll learn from history, though, as those poor, brave souls who came too soon before me could not possibly have done.

Nietzsche's Style. One of the glories of Nietzsche's style is how like marginalia it reads. Throw-away stuff. Graffiti. But, uncanny graffiti, like Blake's gloss on Reynolds. Only instead of two words ("Pure Gold!"), a thousand, so that the text which it comments upon is no longer even necessary.

Comic Writing. "The question of the nature of comic writing is in part a question of aesthetic theory," writes Burgess in an essay on Kierkegaard. To which I would only demur that it is a question of aesthetic theory entirely.

The Next Kafka. I am suspicious of those artists who play to type. Anyone seen sneering around the town in black beret and studded jeans cannot possibly have much sense of the fundamental irony of identity. And without that minimal psychological equipage, what can one really hope to accomplish? Well, yes, an inadvertent parody which one can feign – after the sniggers have died down – having intended all along, but that is hardly *The Divine Comedy* that one sets out toward on the original impulse, is it? The next Kafka will doubtless be some poor soul over-meticulously groomed in what appears to be the cast off clothes of some middle-aged insurance clerk. Just as the last Kafka was.

My Words. I was passing down a crowded downtown street. On my left was a poor, hunched over schlub in ratty clothes, looking worried. "There but for the grace of God go I," I said. Then I realized I was looking at my reflection in a shop front window. "Pull yourself together, man!" I shouted. The wind blew my words out into the street where they were struck by a taxicab.

Minor Works. Dostoyevsky's *The Eternal Husband,* a minor work? By contrasting it to some of his other writings? Surely when you compare greatness to greatness, you still speak only of greatness. The term "minor" ought to be shelved when discussing aspects of so prodigious an oeuvre as that of Dostoyevsky. A 10,000-foot peak is still an awe inspiring sight, whatever Olympian reaches stand near it. In discussing the works of the great ones, ye academicians, let us not forget for a moment who we are, nor upon what plateau we stand.

cf. William Blake's "Book of Urizen," "Book of Thel". All prophetic works are purely personal in their symbology. Some individuals just happen to be microcosms of a larger order. (Might this not be said, as well, for a work like Eliot's "The Wasteland"?)

For You. For you, before there was me, there was the matter of longing to contend with. For me, before there was you, there was the matter of longing to contend with. Blake puts it this way: "What do women in men require? / The lineaments of gratified desire! and What do men in women require? / The lineaments of gratified desire!" If we could conjure from our fancy the proof of our potency. . . . That is to say, if our desire could consume our longing. . . .

Deconstructionism. Everything is reduced to a reflection of the sensibility of its writer. The only escape from this airless ideology is to acknowledge the possibility of a distinction between the writer and the maker. "Romanticist!" You might now cry, if you are attempting to defend your deconstructionist territory against such impossible-to-prove distinctions.

A Zen Address. A Zen address is the only possible refutation of the deconstructive sensibility, in my opinion. Just as the transcendental lyric is the only possible refutation of the ironic sensibility. The refinements of art are, on the one hand, an antidote for the refinements of culture.

The Animating Force. The animating force can only be conceived as a paradox, for wherever it is fixed by perception, it slips to its own shadow.

The Continual Struggle. The continual struggle of the artist to become invisible in his art. As the soul in a man is invisible.

God in Man. God in man is the show stopper, that's all it is. Every holy order is a Broadway production.

The Truth. The truth is afraid of us.

Mozart. I represent myself as an authority, but, in fact, I am merely a disciple. My "personal genius" – if any – derives from an ability to weigh the "dictation" against my own scrupulous observation of what is humanly relevant. It is one thing to make a verbatim transcript from the angel tongue and another to recognize the limitations of the human sense organs. Had we three ears, or even none, it would have been another concerto entirely, according to Mozart.

Gender. None of us can know much more about loving one another than that to which our gender consigns us. This ought not to be true and we would prefer not to believe it, and it may no longer be true tomorrow, but up to this very instant, history has proved it.

Contemplation. Contemplation is spiritual, communication psychological. Explanation is best made by analogy. Flight is best left in the air of its occurrence.

Crisis. If a person has made a firm decision to leave by the door and yet he finds himself at the window, opening it to leap out, that is a crisis of existentialism. Whether or not it is also a question of predestination is a point hardly liable to deduction. My experience, however, has been that conflict of forces from which the individual Will is derived invariably appears to have been merely a "seeming" conflict. There is really only one choice, and that choice is made for us. (That is, to say it bluntly, we have no control over our fate, only over the sensibility with which we engage it.) The artistry of our engagement is the sole measure of our spiritual nature. Out of nothing at all, then, or out of liquid gold, no more nor less is really possible. That is what they call, in the midst of those existential crises, "the crucial issue of faith." My friend, it is best let go of. If you find yourself at a door, step through it; if you find yourself at a window, leap!

II

Books. Books do not contain their authors fully. But, for the most part, what their authors would have themselves taken to be. This is not an intentional deception, but an inevitable one.

As Pie. The character of a work of art is all in its style – not, as the moralizers would wish it, for ease sake, in its content. How easy as pie it would be to make profound art, simply by adding a few choice ingredients: apples for knowledge; peaches for desire. It is all in the mixing, however.

The Purpose. The purpose of art, the purpose of all writing, the purpose of genuine thought, is not to comment upon the past, or to elucidate the present, but to create the future.

Romance. "I am not dangerous to you, of course, so I doubt that you would be interested in me. However, there is always the aspect of you being dangerous to me to add spice to our romance." "Quite enough," she agrees, snuggling up.

The Marketplace. "Where are you off to?" "The whorehouse!" "And then?" "The marketplace!" "What then of honor?" "What then of death!"

Desired. I would rather be desired than respected. In fact, the idea of being respected without some degree of erotic attraction strikes me as vaguely insulting. Speaking here, of course, purely of the respect of women. Of men, I would, rather than their respect, have the assurance that in their eyes, I am a saleable commodity.

A Dialog. "I warn you of my vanity," she says. "And I warn you of mine," I reply. "I warn you of my voracious appetite," she says. "And I warn you of my ability to rise again like a Phoenix," I reply. "I warn you of my love . . . in advance," she says. "And I, of mine . . . in retreat," I reply. Two sword players, we are, hoping against hope for that unexpected, immortal wound.

Specks. "Were you calling me today?" I ask her. Our two specks mingling in eternal space.

Scholarship. The ideal of scholarship is not that it somehow exhaust its subject, but rather that it inspires a furtherance, into that subject, of exploration. All scholarship ends in failure. The extent of that failure is precisely the extent to which it attempts to be exhaustive.

Fallen Stars. How should I be so lucky as to find, among fallen stars, you? How should I have been kicking at the debris, the rubble fallen at my feet, only to unearth, as a diamond glinting out of fired coal, you? How should I of all men, the least loquacious, the most utterly tongue tied, be the one come bearing this poem, to you? My mind is a tangle, how should you be the one who makes it clear again that we are all here, each and every one of us, to live beautiful lives?

Auden and Baudelaire. Auden and Baudelaire on the one hand. Yeats and Blake on the other. Self-contempt is the yin of transcendentalism's yang. In terms of what its highest practitioners produce, there is no distinction. "What self?" as Lao-Tzu said.

Existentialist Principles. Existentialist principles eventuate spiritual convictions, but only after they have been lived through thoroughly. At least that is the idea one gets from reading Kierkegaard, or for that matter Kafka. Autobiography is existential. So is death. Sex, too, but not love. That is to say, women when seen through the window are existential, but not when met at the door. The young are naturally existential. Copious writing is existential, but not when it is covert. That is to say, madness is not existential, but sanity is. The existential tradition is essentially a tradition of "humanism." Schweitzer was an Existentialist. All western medical practitioners are. That is to say, the body is existential.

The Service of Existentialism. In the existential tradition, all service to humanity is simply an inadvertent by-product of the perpetual examination for motive that constitutes the existential stance. That is to say, the Existentialist cannot achieve a state of sainthood, save by service to the self. For which reason it has a tradition of ironists, though emphatically not a tradition of cynics. I have heard it described as "darkly optimistic."

Tradition. In the existential tradition, it is not so necessary to believe oneself to be just, as to act with what one believes to be justice. Existentialism has that in common with the Zen tradition: an impeccable sense of its aesthetic sensibilities. The Zen spirit of existential tradition, did I say? Indubitably!

III

Hesse. "Your destiny loves you," wrote Hesse. Destiny will defer to the will of the individual, but not necessarily to that individual's betterment. Free will, indeed, is something to be used sparingly.

Roman Empire. I was involved in something like this before and it was...fabulous! Until, of course, it fell, as all fabulous things must, to ruin. She was my Holy Roman Empire.

It Occurs. It occurs to me that the reason I am treated as one bound to the standard contract of my social environment is that I represent myself as someone bound to the standard contract of my social environment. No brilliant deduction, this, I realize, but does no one recognize the possibility that I have privately appended a clause? Surely a poet, of all the creatures on God's grey earth, is not to be taken at face value. Why, indeed then, would he be a poet at all, if he really meant himself to be just another bad actor?

Horror and Astonishment. "Imagine my horror and astonishment," writes Charles Baudelaire. And, knowing him well enough, I read no further. No wonder he had such an affinity for Edgar Allen Poe, in whom, too, the astonishment of horror was of endless allure.

Pensées. It doesn't matter, just so long as it is the *pensées* of some French Existentialist, the way I am absorbing ideas and spitting out corollaries. I am like a factory that refines pearl dust into gilt-edged clouds.

Biography. There is nothing more sinister to me than literary biography, unless it be the deconstruction of the artistic "personality" by principles of psychology. What could be less illuminating of the poetry of Baudelaire than a Freudian analysis of his character? Why not a tarot card reading, or critique by Ouija board?

IV

Principles of the Absurd. By one way of looking at it – that is, with regard to posterity – I have made nothing but a series of successful decisions. But would I want to repeat my life over again? Exact in every detail? That is what is known as a question of the absurd. The absurd is an achievement not for the one who does the achieving, but for everyone else. For example, Sisyphus endlessly rolling his stone almost to the peak of the hill, only to have it roll back down again so that he must start over. That is an achievement for all mankind. Well, why not? The absurd is a "religious" achievement in the sense that it negates the individual personality. The existential is a psychological achievement, or an achievement in philosophy, in the sense that it augments the individual personality. The highest act of existentialism is always an attainment of the absurd, whereas the highest act of absurdity is an attainment to the state of sainthood. Again, let us define the absurd as an achievement, the ramifications of which are unknowable. The artist of the absurd is so sane in the largest sense as to be pragmatic even about the dissolution of his own mind. It is this pragmatism that separates him from the estate of the madman – who occupies the same province, but without the same equanimity.

Potboilers. I wonder, could one consider Herman Hesse's *Siddhartha* a Buddhist "potboiler?" Not at age twenty-three, certainly, but at age forty-three, perhaps. All of Dostoyevsky's works are, of course, potboilers, with the exception of his

Siberian prison camp memoir, *The House of the Dead*. Sinclair Lewis? The Nobel Prize for pot-boiling. Jean Rhys? *After Leaving Mr. Mackenzie; Good Morning Midnight*. I mean, come on! All the best of writing is tripe and sentimental hogwash. So, too, all the best of ourselves.

In Their Longing. In their longing for one another, they invent themselves and allow others to invent them, but – and this is the real issue at the core of existentialism – in too much haste. It is all invention and being invented by, but the star that hangs over the personality of genius is patience.

More Separate, More Alone. I feel myself becoming more separate, more alone, with every passing day, but the only despair I feel with regard to this is that it does not happen quickly enough. (However, I would not like it to be said that my appreciation of things sensual is diminishing – only my sense of the over-riding importance of such things.)

Dylan Thomas. "The force that through the green fuse drives the flower/drives my green age," wrote Thomas. Every spring, I am loath to turn away from myself to the more ungraspable miens of the world unbounded.

Servitude. We have become so habituated to our servitude as, say, with the condition of gravity, that we still are able to imagine ourselves as some kinds of masters. Case in point: the iron rule of the king.

My Dealings with Women. In my dealings with women, I am profoundly unresourceful, although the fact that I am married does, necessarily, inhibit the possible scope of my offerings, especially with regard to that most precious commodity of seduction: time. When poor SK set out to seduce Cordelia, he had money, time and wit. It was, of course, the wit that undid him. "My Dear Cordelia," he wrote, and every agency of the earth, sky and underworld sat up to take notice of the play about his lips.

Nietzsche's Expression. The genius that predominates in Nietzsche, the one that defines him, is not the genius of ideas, but the genius of expression. It is a mistake, therefore, to think that one understands Nietzsche simply because one shares his views. Even poor Nietzsche could not understand this, or would not allow himself to believe it, especially with regard to his beloved, unattainable Lou Andreas Salome. No, by no means did she understand him. Her poor prose was plodding, plodding.

Lou Salome. The psychological "insights" that a person like Salome could have had into a person like Nietzsche are so fraught with the issues of power and need that revolved around their personal relationship as to render them effectively irrelevant with regard to his historical situation as a "lover of wisdom," except in the frivolous biographical terms of dramatic personae.

Lucid Despair. Believe me, it is not lucid despair that arises from the depths of "real" misery, but inarticulate despair. Anytime a precise metaphor arises spontaneously out of a work of seeming pessimism, you can be sure the artist is in a condition of creativity far removed from the issues of "apparent personal happiness" and "positive self-image." Nietzsche, in that case, is like the Samurai who, falling upon his own sword, achieves salvation.

Diffidence. It is one thing to be diffident about talent if you have none, but if you have talent and are diffident about it, that is another issue entirely. (cf. The uncanny diffidence of Kafka, of Kierkegaard.) When authors of this caliber evince skepticism as to the ultimate value of their literary achievements, without any coy denials of their sublime literary abilities, it is hard not to take notice. The self-deprecation of such authors are often termed "wry," when in fact they are quite literal. "As against God," wrote Kierkegaard, "we are always in the wrong." And one might wonder if after he coined this, he did not whisper: "Even me, Lord?" And hearing the response affirmative, put down his pen without adding any subjunctive. Is it the other end of this spectrum whereon Knut Hamsun, upon hearing he had been awarded, at age eighty, the Nobel Prize, mutters, "They should have given it to me thirty years ago, when I could have used it"? Or is that, too, an example of sublime diffidence, but carried out in a more complex, psycho-theatrical mode? The author owes to his readership the best that he is able to give. However, whether his readership has any exterior existence begs the question of artistry as if it were one of metaphysics.

The Afterworld. Imagine if I were to meet in the afterworld someone whose reputation I had defamed, solely for the sake of making a very original point that few enough would ever read, let alone understand. Let me put it this way: I will forgive all those who defame me, so long as the lyric of their aspersion is fit.

Last Night, a Thousand Poems

Spirits. People to whom the spirits sing should not be so proud. To be so near death is not to expand life, but to worry it into a sort of crystal.

And as for the Enlightened. And as for the enlightened, one can only pity them the deceptions of their muses. I say this with all due respect to those who do not care what I say and so have truly passed beyond me. I used to be enlightened myself, but it was a case of mistaken identity. It turned out to be somebody else. Still, there must be those in the world who are above it all. Those who pass among us like clouds, changing shape to suit the wind, as would befit a person of true humility. I met a man once who could read minds. He looked into my eyes and said, "You are very, very ignorant." No wonder we begrudge these Ubermench their say and call them mad. They hold such unpopular opinions. The question of enlightenment has always concerned me. Considering the state that the world is in, I think it is safe to say that the smart people are simply not smart enough. They just have their ways of getting things done. And the rest of us can't dispute them, because they hold so tenaciously to their logic. They have their Ph.D.'s tattooed to their foreheads, some of these imbeciles. But, who then are we supposed to trust? If intelligence is insufficient and genius is so harsh? Should we turn the reins over to the mentally retarded? At least they won't be building us any ballistic missile silos. If it were up to me, the people who ruled the world would be the people who least wanted to do it. You'd have to track them down to their grass huts for consultations on the affairs of state and you might find them there, sipping tea and thinking wistfully of simpler times. You might say to them, "What about the poor?" and they might respond, "Have them send all their money to me."

Wouldn't it be nice to hear something illogical once in a while from those dried out sticks whom we have allowed to procure positions of high authority? Something entirely spontaneous? Soon we'll have actual wooden puppets in our White House and in our state mansions. Or computer read outs. Give me a person with a mirror for a face, any day. At least you know he'd be accessible to that particular moment in time and not merely a statue with a point of view.

One Minute. One minute I am here, the next minute I am there, with you. One minute I am earthbound and the next I am on a train. One minute I am blind and the next I have seen glory. One minute I am mute and the next I am singing hallelujah! One minute I am one and the next I have become a chorus. But that is just what the poems are written to shake away, my friends: the sense that one belongs in this world to anything but the tumbling dice.

Poetry. Poetry is a surprising sport. One often flushes the jester from the meadow when one is chasing butterflies. A poem should be no longer than the person who writes it. Over emoting when reciting a poem is like shouting "bang!" when you fire off a pistol. I really don't believe in long poems. I believe in very, very short poems. I believe that long poems are simply short poems that missed their turnoffs a ways back and are too proud now to stop and ask for directions. Some poets right boats that should be sunk. This is called false metaphor, when the place looks full that is really empty.

Sensuousness. Men wrapped up in sensuousness should forego the urge to write poetry, as should women wrapped up in men. The latter is a pudding to be supped. The former is a prong to be staked. Poetry does not result directly from feelings, but from the poet's unavailing resistance to such.

Pen and Sword. It's true, the pen is mightier than the sword, but after all, only cloud shapes are distinguishable in that statement. I have known poets who thought they wielded broad-axes when they rhymed aptly. Poetry is a place for the grandiose to escape into, all right. A never-never land in which the foolish can remain forever young.

A Petal. When one peels a petal from the temple wall, innocence blinds. Seek only, rather, to know the trance of power that is in the hearts of the pure.

Vendetta. An artist who says he has no vendetta is lying to himself and deluding no one. Even the great sages were at war with the heavens, if only on our behalf. Wisdom is to struggle not for oneself, but for others.

The Mask. The mask of true art is a crass professional who has somehow subdued the Gods.

The Task. Here is a task for a writer: to erect a wall between one's self and the sky, and to write upon it – aye! – with the stars showing through.

Futility. There is so much futility among the poets. But let us not deprecate the value. Futility is an inverted charm; it lets us see what we would be if we were not striving.

Both. The poet is both a mask and a revelation.

Nonsense. The predilection for nonsense is a nice touch in a poet. Alas, seldom seen, rarely heard, the worm turning in the core of the moon.

Parable. A poet came to a well in which the stars were reflected and he lowered his cup into it and he raised the cup and he drank from it. Lo! His face was burning and he said, "I have not had so great a thirst as this in a thousand years." So, he lowered his cup again into the well and again he drank from it, and now his face shone like a beacon. He said, "I grow thirstier still," and again he drank, and now he glowed like an angel and he said, "I shall enter this well," and he plunged bodily into it and he sank like a stone, drinking as he fell. And lo! Many years passed before another poet came to the same well and he dipped his cup into it and what do you know? Up came the first poet crying, "Desist! For I am drinking here." "That is all very well," said the second poet. "But, it seems to me that you have all the water that you need." At this, the first poet smiled. "All the water that I need would not fill a thimble," he said. "Then why," asked the second poet, "do you drink here and tell others that they may not?" The first poet laughed. "Why not ask the sky?" he said. So the second poet turned to the sky, shaking his fist, and demanded to know the answer. "All immensity could not fill this poet," the sky replied. "For he is dead and the well is tainted." "Now do you understand?" the first poet asked. "I have not been wise," the second poet bowed. "I am indebted."

The Sun. It is a rare day that the sun does not shine somewhere. Let it be life itself, then, and not the place from which one is looking.

An Angel. It may not be possible to remain an angel after a certain point, but one can always be a fool. After innocence vanishes, all that remains is understanding.

My Sex Life. My sex life is a departed bus. I'll say no more about this; only that I have had and I have had not, and to have is better than to tip one's cap to the queen of the angels.

Freedom. About freedom, there is only this: what is the point? At a certain hour the bells toll for all of us. Free persons upon the earth? This is not a home, but the birthplace of forgetting.

Reaping. I'm all for reaping what I sow, except as it be sowed upon me. The question of will is the question of human nobility.

A Culture. A culture is the artifacts of reasoning. What pompous statements will our passage make to the archeologists of the future? Here is a battlefield upon which many were lost?

Justice. I'll allow for the divinity of justice, but not for its explication.

Proof. Proof is the burden that we have thrust upon one another's ideals. If this is not enough said, I will only add: there is no time for proving we are who we dream we are; there is barely enough time for dreaming.

Earth. Earth is an involuntary activity of exploration. It is mostly breathing. Those of us who can spend the next millennium as fish will probably have a better chance of surviving the next millennium.

Pleasure. One finds pleasure in the bearing out of effort, and one exercises will over pleasure as best as one can.

A Dogma. The relevance of any dogma is attested to by its disciples, but the relevance of any disciple is a question at hand.

Student. The student will worship, but refrain from judging him on the slackness of his jaw. Seek, rather, his inner wording, and look for that listening that speaks. The lantern above a student's desk is first a moon before it is a sun.

Zen. In teaching, teach! In learning, learn! In seeking, seek! It is one world after another, all in the same place.

A Teacher. A teacher says to his student, "Take care, take heed. It is one march to destiny and another to the fife and drum."

A Thousand Poems. In Zen antiquity there is a poem, "Last night, a thousand poems. Who can understand me?" If these are the words of a sage and I know what they mean, what does that say about wisdom? That it is too easily conceived? Or is it only that I have, myself, a touch of moonlight in my veins. Even after all the pains my society has taken to make me technologically culpable. No matter. I hope all is going well for you, too, and that the muse has not left you bereft simply because of your implicit disbelief. Like a good friend, a good angel is not easily dissuaded. As Basho wrote:

> To the willow –
> All hatred, and desire
> Of your heart.

The Attributes of Zen Poetry. The attributes of Zen poetry are: good nature, objectivity and charm. Now, charm is of an entirely different order than wit. Charm wins by losing. Particularly with Zen haiku, it is important not to overstate one's emphasis. A flower is not a sword, though some of us it reaps as finely. One needs to be prepared to die into the moment.

> A peony!
> As white . . .
> As the moon.

From there, it is but one leap to the sun.

> A Chinese rain!
> All flowers
> Growing tall.

Empty Throne. Art is an existing excellence, not an empty throne. There is no succession more foolishly conceived than the temporal. Current Poet Laureate of the Library of Congress notwithstanding – naturally!

One's Master. One's master never changes, though the face be rearranged. A poet who does not love poetry itself takes the devil for a fool.

What to Fear? Fear no evil. It is only the loss of one's aesthetic that one must fear.

Follies. Who know what protects us from our follies? Our illusions may protect us more than our reason. Illusion and reality are so often contradictory, that one cannot help but suspect that they are two aspects of the same vision.

Paradox. Paradox is the birth into space of time. To come full circle is not as much of an accomplishment as is to end up in a different place. That is what the snake eats: the accomplishment of reason and the foundation of order – or, in other words, his own tail.

The Queen Bee of Fairyland

The Queen Bee of Fairyland. Kierkegaard was in my head a lot that year. At the library, next to Nietzsche's, I stared at Kierkegaard's collected works the most. In opening at random to a passage, I usually found a sentiment concurrent with my own. How I coveted his succession: *Fear and Trembling; The Sickness Unto Death.* Only Baudelaire's *Les Fleurs De Mal* made more of a neurotic impression on my hitherto neo-classical, mountain-topping, hearty-Germanic temperament. Melancholia was an exercise I indulged in, but I did not dwell in the house of dim light for long without regretting some irretrievable loss of sunshine and of meadow. My girlfriend was a pensive violet, opening only by night and I thought that her poems were remarkable. It was one morning in a coffee shop, after bingeing on champagne, that I looked at her and vowed eternal love. "Swear it by the Queen Bee of Fairyland," she said. I did. Her poems were both romantic and disconsolate: wine-purple flowers calling down from the sky. "The sun is setting," I often thought when I looked at her, "and soon we will be lost in our promises." Kierkegaard wrote, "A vow broken is twice a vow." And so it is. Once going and once coming, the promise is fully formed of its splendor.

Writing. I enjoy writing. It is a pastime for me. I do not understand those who obsess over it. To me, words are playthings. A convenient place to draw one's bath. If it is derelict to have a high style, it is positively egocentric to not exist at all. Should the mockingbird stammer just because somewhere an angel sings so beautifully he is bringing down the very throne of God? One does what one can. That is both will and wisdom. And where the twain are met, there grow trees of gemstones, wine and flowers. Ah, indeed, paradise.

Two Men. Two men were standing at a crossroads. One said to the other, "When paths cross again, be there." "I am," the other said.

A Dog. A dog found a diamond and he took it home to his master. "Good boy!" his master said, and he gave the dog a bone for his trouble. "If I had known that was all I was going to get for it," the dog growled, "I would have eaten it myself."

A Poet and a Priest. A poet and a priest were out walking on the beach one afternoon. The poet noticed that the priest was leaving no footprints. "That is a shame," the poet said. "It is not I who am with God, but you are," the priest replied.

Death. "There is no death," said the watchman. "And the proof is that I have killed him. I slew him with my sword as he was entering the gates of the city, riding on a black horse." "That was not death," chimed the bell tower. "That was only death's shadow." "Where then can death be found?" cried the watchman. "In the place where he has fallen, he stands mourning," chimed the bell tower.

The Old Days. In the old days, when a man died, his shadow was boxed up and sent to his nearest living relative. "What shall I do with this?" the son asked, when his father's shadow arrived. "Make of it a garment for your life," his wife replied.

Marriage. Marriage is a ceremony of innocence. If a man were to ask his wife on their wedding night, "Are you a virgin?" It is well that she might answer in truth: "Yes, twice."

Parted. Two men met again at a crossroads. "We have never parted," said the one. "Until before now," said the other. One stepped back into the mirror, and all was lost.

On Arthur Rimbaud. Rimbaud was a fallacy created by Rimbaud. "I is another." He said it best, himself. But what does it mean? Not merely disintegrating self-reflection, but actual spirit possession. So it goes! One does not always know the consequences of one's actions, but if one can apprise oneself of the terrain, one might guess the manner of being who might be met there. There is always an entrance to the underworld. Heaven's gate, however, is not so easily shaken.

True. It is not true that all writing is folly. What is true is that all writing which does not explicate itself is fallacious. The tendency of postmodern writing toward obsessive self-annihilation is not a *reductio ad absurdum,* but merely a thought experiment gone awry by virtue of the imperfect medium of its transmission. No one said it was going to be easy. Such experiments really ought to be carried out in a more physical medium. Absurdity would be joyously dancing one's self to death. No dream ever defined.

Two People. Two people are arguing over an empty box. Their struggle is its only content.

On a Book of German Fairy Tales. A moral is a way of impeding the story while appearing to complete it. Conclusions are always fatuous, often false. No end is complete but by paradox.

Let the Giant. Let the giant weep waterfalls. Suffering is acute enough without bombast. The truly damned are rarely rich rhetoricians. It is the angels in their falls who speak so delusively, and of a place to which they have not yet come.

The Years. The years of solitude may not pass so glowingly as the night of dreaming. There is yet time to kiss the wife, though the angel seizes you by the short hairs. Which of us know the power of his own mercy? It may yet redeem the one who bestows it.

House and Key. One person has a house to which there is no key. Another has a key to which no door can be found. Try though they might, they can be of no use to one another. The house is called Parting. The key is called Mind.

Chinese Antiquity. Chinese antiquity has given us nothing more than Chinese antiquity. However, that is still far more than our own age has given us. The poems of the T'ang, of the Ming, of Lao-Tzu and of Chuang-Tzu; these are notable for their lack of pretension. The nobility of their simple presence speaks for itself, as well as for things far greater. A mountain is contained in the palm of a hand. A fish swims in moonlight. As well in, as out of mind, these things are conceived. Chinese antiquity has shown us a pathway to the Soul. Are we to slough off such gestures as trivial, simply because they are tiny? Faith is a seed, after all, and not a tree. How big does it need to be?

Criticism. The poet is best served by criticism who holds a double dose of classical scholarship close to his vest. Criticism is not negation, although affirmation of negation it may be. The cynic must hold the lightest pen. Who wields the torch that sets the blaze must have the easiest conscience. In point of fact, the poet is the genius of his age. One may not recognize him by his face or manner, for genius is always in advance, and his face is the face of the future. What is invisible today will tomorrow be made plain. Books are the key. Those who do not read, cannot see. Where the blind felicitate one another on their clear-sightedness, there, indeed, is hell.

The Apple. Where the apple hangs from the tree, there we are, and there the universe is.

A Clear Mind. A clear mind is necessarily better off than a deep mind; for objects, when they are truly weighted, will continue to fall. I have my definition of the word beautiful; it is: to make exact. What is made plain is simple in many dimensions. Time contained by mind.

Dreaming. Dreaming, one sees what ought to be light in what ought to be darkness. Such as is contained in our understanding, is the extent to which we can express its beauty. As the flower expands, so must the fruition.

Proportion. Beauty is in proportion. Time is in relation.

Vanity. It is vain to propound. Vainer still to fail to elucidate.

Oh, Yes. Oh, yes, or dream yourself away, if you can, from the marriage bed where the wolf bares his teeth at the lamb and says, "Innocence is slander."

The World. The world is wrong. That is what we fall in love to defend against.

Sunken Ships. Not too great a day, really, but at least I am free to make my own choices. I have a good wife and a lovely child. The important thing is that I am not in jail. Do the imprisoned wander the streets alongside me, on any given day? You know that they do. Men and women, bound hand and foot, have entered even this establishment where I now dine. They have sat, ordered, eaten, got up, and left, never realizing that the bearing walls have given way and they are drowning in their chains. Each of us is a deep sea. A self can so quickly become a sunken ship.

The Done Deed. Does the done deed remain done past the time of its doing, or is it ever undoing? Constant vigilance! How much wood could a woodchuck chuck if a woodchuck could chuck wood? Always double check for clarity. That is the correct answer to that.

The Invisible. Without the invisible, there could be nothing upon which to compose.

A Miracle. A miracle is worth all the painful reasoning that leads up to it.

God and Devil. Good and evil are much to decide of an act, the consequences of which we know not what force exerts.

The Judge. When the judge descends, the arbiter expands. Freedom is timelessness.

Molecules and Atoms. Molecules and atoms are more accessible than reason, because molecules and atoms actually exist, whereas reason is an illusion of context. That which does not choose its own time to change, eternity will amend. That is known as Free Will. The freedom to do what must be done.

When That. When that which had been created unconsciously begins to be created consciously, then the art is creating the artist, and the cycle is complete.

Struggle. Do not struggle over your writing. The struggle will form. Hold the pen loosely. It is a mind which you hope to impose upon the page, not a musculature. Where heart and mind are not in union, there can be no poetry. Words, then, this bridge between me and thee, are equally task and master.

True Bride. All communication is collaboration. The listener has to want to understand the speaker. The speaker has to want to be understood. An archer, sighting his target, might miss up and then down, right and then left, before finding the bull's eye. Just as the eternal groom in search of his true bride.

A Star. Are even the Gods content just to dream? A wish that has been granted is empty. A star is aspired.

Weird Emptiness

Notes on Vocation. Roof repair guy came over again today to nail back down the shingles that had been pulled up by the recent winds. He's a sparkly, sprightly, early sixty something year old, with deep lines drawn in his face by a lifetime of skepticism and ribaldry. The main thing about him, his name is Jerry, he's independent. A handyman, self-employed, and successful enough that he does not return calls promptly. "Alex Stein!" he cries into the phone. "Jerry Dickinson." "Jerry," I cry back. "Good to hear your voice, sir!" And it really is. He seems something to me of a familiar. I am not ribald, but I am skeptical. To be ribald would require a philosophical fatalism that my experience of the world has precluded. One must be free to be fatalistic. A poet may be many things, but a poet is never free. I am driving down the highway to the University of Denver, talking into a handheld tape recorder. The clouds are like luminous throw rugs, tossed here and there by some gargantuan decorator God to break up the sky.

Strangers. It is only in the communion of spirits that nothing is lost or left behind. Between you and I, what the gap of even a day might bring is enough to make strangers of us. This is either an argument against relationship at all or an argument, perhaps – and I can't believe I am already thinking this – for marriage in the most traditional sense of the term.

Wine or Adulation. I am educated. In fact, I am in the process of becoming very highly educated. Thinking is something that I happen to do well without much exertion, so I have found myself, serially, in situations that depend for their success on the vigor, the temerity, the originality, of my intellect. What suits me about the intellectual life is not its isolate condition, but the company it keeps. Artists are oddities and – if one looks past some of the more egregious of their eccentricities (the habitual arrogance, for example) – they are engaging oddities. Under the influence of wine or adulation even the most austere of them can become endearingly childlike.

Into the Garden. I don't condone generalities. They are a form of dissimulation, but in general my temperament is one of equanimity and my aspirations are one with what they have been in humankind since Adam first entered out from the void and into the Garden.

Maelstrom. I'm bang-smack in the middle of one of those moronic literary maelstroms. Those tempest in a teapot feuds that go on in the halls of academia where, as my friend Fred Baca puts it, "The responses are so exaggerated because the stakes are so low." Once there were herds and herds of wild horses in this country. Now there are only corrals, and a few sodden creatures of pale remembrance prancing in their halters.

Conditions. There is no condition that cannot be overcome. It is this to which the comics allude, when they long, in the midst of their comic conundrums, an interminable evening at the opera, let us say, for "the sweet embrace of death." Life is sweet, but only in its distillation, only in its essential qualities. The well-spring is deep, its waters are dark, and madly, maddeningly, like a damsel in a beach bikini, it has hidden its fount in plain view. So long as one is involved in the question of apportioning out blame, there is no prospect of forward motion. Two large stones on a scale: one will not be made the lighter if one paints on its outer surface, "the lighter," any more so than the other will be made significantly the heavier by painting on its outer surface, "the heavier."

Sluice. It's like there is this sluice in my head through which all the information is sifted except a few golden nuggets which I retrieve and burnish.

Psychic Phenomena. I had no alternative but to study psychic phenomena. The critical events in my life were all psychic in their manifestations.

1984. In 1984, in Seattle, my teacher came to me. I did not know that I was quote ready unquote. "What do you want from me?" I asked. "It is so beautiful to be free," he replied, wrapping the first of many chain loops around me. "I shall make you free."

All I Asked. All I ever asked of my teacher was that he not make himself mysterious to me. "I never will," he laughed. "And if you were funny," I added, "that would be good, too." He winced. "Let's begin with your poetry," he sighed. "It stinks."

Without a Master. It is hard to write poetry without a master. In fact, it is hard to do anything transcendental without a master. Willpower and determination are beautiful things but without access to the spirit realm, the creative will eventually bow down to the demands of the prosaic, claiming for a rationale that suspiciously supercilious term, "pragmatism." The spiritual is not a kind of idealism, it is a kind of fundamentalism. Our breath, for example, and to put it in the most basic terms possible, is spiritual.

1988. In 1988, I lived by the water and I communed on marsh banks with cat-tails and butterflies. I was so damn pure in myself that it was like nothing to sleep with my girlfriend in the afternoon and then to go home and sleep that same night with my wife. It is hard to recreate such purity. Everything else can be recreated, but not purity. At least, not so easily. I do remember that the angle by which I had to enter into my girlfriend was oblique to the angle by which I was used to entering into my wife. I doubt I had much understanding of the power of a stimulated clitoris with regard to either of them, but in me at least, between them, something was fully consummated. My teacher's take on sex was that it was not all that important. In that regard, he was not wrong, exactly, but certainly misleading. Or, rather, he was not wrong about its importance to me, but if he was so all-knowing, wouldn't you think he might have made some mention of the hysteria it would arouse in others?

Recollections from the Life of an Acolyte. "It is not enough to act with humility," our teacher said. "One must actually be humble. This is a stricture that will be harder to adhere to, the more spiritual insight you accrue, but this is the sole stricture upon which you base your vow. There are other monasteries, of course," he added. "But not, though, for any of you. Projecting yourselves into the future, you might ask, 'But how, oh, Master, shall I maintain my humility when I know more than anyone around me?'" He paused. "Ah, then, when that becomes the case you will simply have to will yourself to know less. And if you wish to remember it like this, projecting yourselves, as I say, into that future time, remember, it will not be out of your knowledge that you make of yourself a light."

The Sun. The sun is setting like a giant doubloon, into a trough overflowing with yellow coins. This is what is meant by the richness of the light: this golden ship that rides on the heart-waves that crest the heart's ocean surface.

Zen Mind. The Zen mind is a fortress. The Zen mind is an archer upon a parapet. The Zen mind is an arrow. A pierced heart. Blooming, as it were, in its wounding. It is not necessary to forgive one's enemy. One must only forgive the wound.

"Here," the master says, touching a forefinger to the breast-bone above his heart. "Here is where I have been outraged."

Physical Space. Physical space, mutual shared objective reality is paradigmatic. That is to say it is relational, schematic, contextual. Our activities as physical beings are constrained by the conditions of that paradigm. Including, for starters, the pertinent laws of physics, and the cultural biases of the epoch at issue. That is, for example, to say that, at one level, rebellion, in artistic form, for example (cf. Dada, Surrealism etc.) is as much a creation of the rebel as it is of the oppressor. The "pure" creative act neither intends nor achieves, it simply "is." And, in fact, even that little verb bears on its back the shadowy, the oppressive, dichotomy of what "is not."

II

Plato. The mistake I keep making is in thinking that people are rational, and by rational I mean they recognize that their system of reasoning is purely a product of personal will and not some cosmological *a priori* into which they possess a prophet's insight. The thing is, they speak with such clarity, and convey themselves with such certainty, like broadcast news anchors. While I know nothing but the shadow of what beauty tells.

Textual Note. To lay bare the process of the creative act can only serve to deepen the mystery of its emanation.

Weird Emptiness. Thinking does not occur independent of an objective, but thought does. The mind of God is like a clock, only with neither hands nor a face.

Who Really? Who really believes that erotic exploration is self-derogatory? And if so, with what "higher" activity ought it to be opposed? Spiritual exploration, presumably!

That road in the darkness to nothing, nothing, nothing at all.

Charisma. If anyone ever asked what I would exchange for "charisma" – and I mean real charisma, I mean rock and roll charisma – I would tell them "my common sense," because anyhow, that seems to be the standard bargain.

Space. If we can walk through space, we can certainly walk through time. That is to say, if we exist at all, we exist as well as flying horses and as falling stars.

Who I Am. The question of who I am must at every moment depend upon the context in which I occur. Or should I say: the context in which "I" occurs? But, let me not reduce to a level of mere semantics this most crucial issue of 21st century Being. I is flux. I is oceanic. And, like an ocean, I is still at some far point bounded. I may be even a universe (though of multifarious expression – of life studies and abstracts) yet is still of one mind. It is not expression out of which identity is created, but that out of which expression arises. More substance than shadow is in us, my tangled friends, no matter how the latter may multiply.

Leanne. "Dramatic costumery and accoutrement, including coiffure (not to mention 'attitude'), implies more of a senti-mental than a radical relationship to identity," he said to the spike-haired lesbian. To which she replied, "Oh, yes, unless it's totally an ironic commentary on the eye of the beholder." "How beautiful that is, then," he murmured.

The Other Half. Leanne believes herself to be a great poet, which is half the battle. The other half is to convince every-one else.

Politics. Explication, except between loved ones, is almost invariably cynical. That is to say: political.

Letter from Adam. "Can there be anything more terrible than to be deceived? Self-deceived, I mean. Than to deny the deception? The self-deception, I mean. To live in hope against one's own secret knowing? Can there be anything more terrible than that? Oh, yes, there can. To live without hope. To live in knowing. To live without the self-deception with which God has fortified us. No, my friends, it is not a lesson, this life, it is simply a condition. There are no implications to our acts, there are only acts. Oh, God! Oh, terrible, terrible God of knowing. Return us to our Paradise. Return us to our innocence. Oh, God, oh, God, oh, terrible, terrible God of our knowing, if you won't return us to our Eden, at least, then, return us to our Eve."

Groundwater. What if it were the case that happiness is the groundwater of human existence and bury it though we try, it will still come burbling back up through the cracks to the surface? That would be something of a reassurance during the dark days, now wouldn't it? (And what if just the opposite were true and it was as the Buddha said: "All existence is suffering." What then? Hypocrite! That you would keep a stable of horses and not let them run is simply asinine!)

Graduate School. Not being graduate school material is, for me, sort of like not being beautiful: something that I had long gotten over. Or thought I had. In fact, no one can be immunized against the prick of vanity or ambition. One might be the apostle of Christ and still succumb to the temptation of being mistaken for Him in twilight in a crowded market place.

For Sale. It's all for damn sale, ain't it, man? Even the deep mind of the artist wants its devil contract for deigning to surface. "I'm sure the Lord had his reasons for taking my husband away from me," says the widow, "and depriving my two children of their father." "No doubt," the priest mumbles, mechanically. Although under no foreseeable condition could he imagine a deity who at this late epoch attached any significance at all to life or to death.

Our Age. Writer after writer, they set forth on one impossible journey after another. That is to say, they set forth without hope, without charity, without faith in themselves, and without Gods. And when they fail to attain their alleged ends they say to have proven by these failures the irony of seeking. Alas, all they have proven is the irony of setting forth without hope, without charity, without faith in oneself and without Gods. The sort of ship that one sails is not immaterial to the sort of sea that one sails it upon.

Trouble. Poetry is in serious trouble. Even the people who write it will barely (except for a few longtime favorites and the works of their close poet friends) read it. I do not say that this quirk disqualifies them from their chosen avocation, but it would be damn strange if it abetted them.

Addendum. I'm not trying to write anything in particular. Impressions flow into me. Sometimes I enter the world, as through the door of myself. Unfocused, I should say it is, but with faithful abeyance. Heeding, should it come, the distant call that says, "Now. Now is the time. It is the time now. Come to me." It is not, obviously, for everyone, this life. The willful, the immoderate, the prudish. Nor, need I even add, is it a life of clear value. It is a life. That much, and not much more, as can be said for any of us, only, can be said. Just now, the birds are going crazy. I am seated at my desk, looking out the window of my study into the back yard. That is twenty-four more words than this little essay really needed, not counting this sentence, but it is so pleasant to pass the time thus – hoping to strike between pen point and page, a tiny, perfect bloom.

My Point of View as an Author. A truly absurd occurrence is like a religious miracle to me: and it is equally as rare. There is no feigning the semblance of genuine human striving. It is for that reason that the great are less gifted than the good.

III

William Carlos Williams. I fully concur with William Carlos Williams' "deep need to write poems that would *provide me with information* [italics mine] rather than functioning as more or less well crafted reproductions of what I already know." Me? I want to write poetry that cleaves a place in the brain where the new waters can gather.

Robert Duncan. "I want to describe poetry," writes Robert Duncan, "before words or signs." Or after words and signs have faded away and all that remains is the energy that devolves from the achievement of some extraordinary resolution?

Divide. It's the great divide, isn't it? And always has been. Poetry on one side, politics on the other. The individual versus the state. The principle defense of poetry being that poets have rarely destroyed any but themselves. Oh, sure, anecdotal exceptions exist, but not, surely, secret mass burial sites.

Personality. Personality is projected (that is, requires the effort of will) out of the base of identity. The concept of identity is spiritual. By which is meant: it exists without regard to our acknowledgment. Willed acts, even acts of goodness and of charity, are always social acts. Even if Will does not demand acknowledgment, it evokes acknowledgment. This consciousness of having acted is dispiriting, even in – or perhaps one might say especially in – the case of acts of generosity. What then, though? Depend on the spirit?

That the spirit is working through it all, tirelessly, invisibly? How? In the face of what horrors come daily? How? Faith and trust? Are these not just more luxuries for those who dwell already fat in mansions?

Ambition. It is a difficult thing to have ambition. It is a bit like keeping a monkey. Also in that it becomes more and more resembling of oneself.

If. If the gods exist, then it does not matter whether or not this is something that one knows.

Phoenix. I am tired of getting older and wiser. I'd like to become younger and to know less. These lines are for you, my dear, and for all those who decry the artistic imperative of self-immolation. As if to be a Phoenix were not the very principle upon which the excursion was founded.

Humor. All humor is based in logic. Even in the case of the absurd there must be some sense that is not being made. Anything can be made disjunctive, but not all *non sequitur* is humorous. Just as much of self-abasement is sheer narcissism.

Originality. Anyone can be original, but in poetry oughtn't that to be just one virtue among many? What the experimental poets pride themselves on is all well and good – but it is not butter and jam for the bread, nor even the bread. What is it, then? It is a recipe for roasted rubber chicken with a side dish of baked soap.

Quicksilver. I must have had a little too much to drink last night because I found myself defending the poetics of Wordsworth to a scion of postmodernism. Which is utterly untenable. Like defending squirrels to foxes. The lines of ordination are just too disparate. J. was drunk, too. She quoted Salinger's observation that childhood is the last time anyone looks good asleep with their mouth open. We made a list of our favorite words. J. liked "cootchie," which is slang for vagina. No one liked "moist," except on the side of a box of cake mix. We were about evenly divided over the word "pulchritude." Toward the end of the evening, J. sat right next to me on the narrow stairway. I was thinking so many things, but mostly: How simple happiness! How fleet! How light! How bold! How like a winged messenger it comes! Like Mercury! Like quicksilver! Like laudanum.

Kafka. The amazing thing about the writing of Kafka is that one can literally see his prose thinking in ways that prose had never before thought, and may never think again. Originality not as an issuance of daring, but as a gift of temperament. Thoroughly unexploitable, incommensurable, inimitable. Kafka is the writer's writer. That is, he is the measure that one takes against one's own writing in terms of its pure connection to the unconscious.

Fauns and Nymphs. Fauns and nymphs. Christ, it has come to this: that the young now appear to me, all and each, as such.

Autobiography. There is nothing to art, nor has there ever been anything to art, except autobiography. And not just in such obvious cases as Saint Augustine or Jack Kerouac, but in every case, not excluding the delusional prophets who believe they preach the word that has been handed down to them from some Other. When a psychologist examines a patient and makes a determination that is a form of autobiography. When an ivory tower poet presumes to "let language speak for itself," even if he or she draws those words at random from a newspaper or has them spit out by a computer program, that is a form of autobiography.

Pedantry. Pedantry is what provokes my ire. The presumption that a thing can be the more dull, the more important that it is. Poetry is poetry when it fails to achieve the one thing that it sets out to do. Otherwise it is merely self-congratulation.

Storehouse of Literature. I have nothing to add to the "storehouse of literature." The deliberate circumscription of my life would prevent me from becoming "universally" relevant, even had I the capacity, but I will say this in defense of my continued production: *cogito ergo sum.*

In Writing. In writing it is sometimes necessary to smudge the details for the sake of form, speed, and what I would call "presence." The quality of presence in writing is approximately what it is in actors: a palpable charisma. However, explication is tedious. A stone is a stone and a bird is a bird. One does not ask a stone to fly nor expect of a bird song that it convey much more than the spirit of its inspiration.

A Poem. "As we are busily building the fortresses of ourselves," says the poet, "the stones have long since fallen. Present acts contain their consequences, as seeds contain their bloom. Full measure has long been taken, so that done and not done are a matter of literal indifference. It is not the journey, but the spirit in which the journey is taken, over which we might exercise some control. The devil may do a deed more glorious than God has ever done, but if it is all for self-aggrandizement, what then?"

Practice. I like the phrase "Buddha consciousness," which according to Ann Charters is Allen Ginsberg's coinage. I like coinage and I guess I'm not totally unimpressed with the conjures of what is called "practice."

Golden Ticket. The works of someone like Allen Ginsberg ultimately fail to satisfy because he has made it too easy on himself. True, no one else can do what he does, but having proved it can be done, what need is there for him to keep on doing it – especially from the individual human spirit evolution standpoint? Unless the poetry is no longer a medium of transformation, but simply the means to an end. Like cash – who cares how it is printed, so long as it spends? And anyway, every poet realizes sooner or later that his work is a sham intended only to aid him in encroaching upon a reality that for one reason or another had been closed to him. "Here is my golden ticket," says the poet, at the gates of the fairground, although it had initially been solely by the eternal glow of his golden being that he had naively hoped to enter.

The Chance. I had the chance, then, to turn my life around before it even got started, had I only known, simply by not doing what I did. We are none of us, though, that rich in prescience (before we have accrued a sufficient capital of hindsight to draw it from). Is there a moment, a single moment, upon which everything hinges? When the screw turns too tight in the bolt and strips the thread? Yes! Just the moment before that. Oh, that time does not move both ways is the sore trial of our human lot.

Facetious. Identity is facetious. Is that the right word? Not farcical, but somewhat of a wry commentary on the ineffable nature of being. One chooses, as such, but whether that choosing is self-willed or pre-determined (to name merely the polar opposites on the spectrum of possibility) is a matter not liable to deduction. You and I might believe that we were born to fall upon one another like dogs and though that belief might be God-like in its prescience, that God – the God of its basis – may still be one of pure subjectivity, and so on, *ad infinitum.* If we cannot even know what we know, can we really imagine to determine who we are? Act then as if how? To which end? In deference, that is, to what ultimate authority? I say this as though your taste was being reckoned along some aesthetic continuum, but that is just me and who, to begin over again, am I?

A Saint. D. says the thing I am writing to, when I think I am writing to her, is really just an idea of her that I have in my mind – which is logical. Bearing in mind that the spiritist will always use the word "logical" with a sardonic inflection. I think about this as I go through my day, the lengths to which any of us will go just to prove to ourselves that our lives have meaning. If – and it must be that it is – this is the purpose to being in love. J. says to me, "Last week I did it with my boyfriend in a church pew," her eyes all aglow with the cruelty of having taken her selfish pleasure. And she, my dear D., I happen to know this for a fact, is in every blessed way a saint.

Principles. In attempting to write essays upon principles of art – which are ultimately metaphysical principles – one comes up against "the paradox of form." Namely that the "full" expression of an idea is inhibited by the material of its expression.

Imponderables. Irreducible dilemmas can be resolved only by inexplicable means – which is to say, by the means of art – which then give rise to their own set of imponderables.

Black Mountain. The activity of the staff and student body at Black Mountain College, which in the late 1950s helped to elevate to public prominence such luminaries as Robert Creeley, Robert Duncan and Charles Olson, was the American movement in poetry most closely related in temperament and sensibility to the Romantic movement in England in the 19th century. Not that any movement need harken back to any other for a measure to be made of its credibility, but it might be an interesting study for some doctoral candidate to graph the parallels that run through the somewhat differing manners of address by which these two groups approach the mysteries of the creative impulse. Am I saying that Olson is Wordsworth, Duncan is Shelley, and Creeley is Keats? Not necessarily. I am merely suggesting that the underlying issues of poetry have remained pretty much constant throughout history and across cultures, and that if one chose to, one might derive from that fact the sense that there could possibly be similarities in other facets of the human sphere of considerations – religion, say, or the construct of society – if one were inclined to such speculations.

A Consideration of "Difficult" Poems. There is, in the philosophy of Zen, a concept of simplicity that is elucidated by the example of a stone tossed into a still pond. It deconstructs like this: the clear enunciation breaks the surface of the mind. Once the surface of the mind has been broken, a succession of ripples accrue, each one broadening the scope of the initial impression. If the universe is curved, as the current popular physics would have it, then eventually the succession of ripples will return to its initiating source. In formal terms, one might say that that return has described the full dimension of that initiating elucidation. From that point, conceptually, it becomes tricky: On the presumption that the ripples do not cease, do they then interact, overlapping themselves, with their own previous evolutionary dispositions? Or do they enter back into their source? In the manner that physics has hypothesized that matter enters into a wormhole, emerging "on the other end" (if that is not too linear a terminology to apply in this instance) to provoke a secondary continuum of evolving ripples still now based upon the initiating source, oddly enough, but with the connection to that source now only as apparent as the connection to the waking life that the sleeper, dreaming, maintains. So, these poetic fragments, these blips, these images, these flashes, these storms, these cross-hairs.

On What Account? If I cannot determine out of what it has arisen, how shall I begin to make any determination at all? And if it is that "a determination" is just what this writing does not ask of me, then how shall I begin to tear my mind away from the reassuring conditions to which it clings? Or, rather, on what account should I?

An Afterthought. Robert Creeley stated at a recent event that "difficult" poetry is about as appealing as difficult love-making, and for approximately the same reasons. A proposition to raise the hackles of the "difficult" poet, don't you know? It has been my experience that every poetic is an afterthought. The necessary Mother, brought in to coddle as much as to condone, the invention that was born almost entirely out of a love for its bearing.

Blake Said. Blake said, "Between true artists there is no competition." Would, perforce, that such a thing said so well were as well done. But there is no sense in mooning about for a world better made than the one we inhabit, now is there?

Fifty Years. If it is simply that the pill is harder to swallow, does that really say anything about the medicine? The poet Mark Irwin once said to me that So-and-So's poems seem difficult to some because So-and-So is writing from fifty years in the future. Most of the poets who are writing and publishing now are writing from fifty years in the past, he said. So, take that, if you like, for your antipode.

Citizens of History

First Breath. A phrase has been running through my head: The Citizens of History. I am thinking of Van Gogh – the emblematic Van Gogh – and others who were without honor in their own time. Nietzsche, in his last correspondences, signed himself, "The Posthumous One." Now there is an ironic twist on the traditional manner of superscription. "What colossal vanity!" the recipients of such missives must have found themselves thinking. But Nietzsche knew it was the people of the future for whom his words were really intended. "Poets and princes," I write (A.D. 2005), "there is a kingdom which persists. Not heaven – imagine that! – but the body of the text returned to its inspiration."

An Artist. An artist died and went to heaven where he was greeted by an archangel who said, "Welcome! I suppose that you have many questions." "What?" the artist replied. "Was my work not good enough to get me damned?"

Friedrich and Sören. Nietzsche was a lyric poet who was also a profound systematic philosopher. Although, not so systematic as some, it goes without saying. The depth of his profundity, his lyric impulse, would not allow it. Kierkegaard was a lyric poet who became a systematic philosopher; achieving in his own lifetime a separation from the lyric impulse. Now, the question is this: which died in madness and which in despair?

Early Writing. When I left home in 1979, I had sure not intended to become a writer, but the Fate which conspired to keep me alone had also – apparently – to be kept regaled. So, write I did. Inauthentically, at first, and then with more and more poise, until I finally had what could be called a tidy box of sums to lay against the time I had spent in their calculation. The actions that we take against our destiny are as raindrops upon the desert, swallowed up in the current of its passage.

Early Writing, Reprised. One of the problems with my early writing (and there were many problems) was that I had not yet learned to let the language think for itself. (I do not, you will notice, say that "I had not yet yielded to its autonomy." That would be a kettle of worms I do not care to pour out.) Rather, I was pressing the language to represent the person who I wished to be taken for. (At times the skin shrinks back from too importunate a touch, but, oh, when it yields to that brute desire and receives us, what a lyrical charge runs through the circuit.)

Baudelaire. Baudelaire's *Paris Spleen* is unquestionably one of the great prose works of the past 200 years. In it, genuine romantic inspiration and the first vestiges of what would eventually be the self-consciousness that would thunder in the era of modernism still cohabitated in a sympathetic mutuality. Not to mention that here was a comic genius of the first order, in consideration of a social milieu (19th century Parisian society), the effete dissipation of which had not been seen since the fall of the Roman Empire. (It is a fortunate thing, indeed, for art, when the body and the priest who attends it, are equally corrupt.)

Paradoxical. In the case of such a paradoxicalist as Baudelaire, one must learn to listen through the seeming point of the exposition to the lyric inflection to derive the unstated irony. Such literature takes a certain amount of patience on the part of the reader, as well as a spiritual affinity. *"Hypocrite Lecteur – Mon Semblable – Mon Frere,"* wrote Baudelaire, in his preface to *Les Fleurs De Mal.* He did not make it easy for us to maintain both our earnest admiration and our political appointments.

The Only Feeling. "The only feeling that convinces me that I am still alive," wrote Baudelaire, "is the vague desire for celebrity, vengeance and money." Hypocritical only in his choice of the adjective "vague." Than this desire, for a poet of such genius and irritability, there can have been none more distinct.

His Ancestors. "My ancestors, idiots or maniacs, in grand apartments, all of them victims of terrible passions," wrote Baudelaire. These "ancestors," of course, were not of the blood, but of the imagination. Biographers who attempt to trace, from his written statements, a family tree, are fools. The father and grandfather of Charles Baudelaire, his uncles and aunts, may not necessarily be the father and grandfather, the uncles and aunts of the narrator of *Le Spleen de Paris.* The texts of certain kinds of literary persons are identities unto themselves; with a genealogy quite distinct from that of their authors. And, it may well be, a distinct psychopathology, as well.

Photographs. It is difficult for me even to look at the extant photographs of Charles Baudelaire. The tight-set, thin-lipped mouth. The resolute stare of authority. This derided man, impotent in his own age, gazing into posterity as if he knows had we been there with him at that time, neither would we have tried to save him.

The Hangman. The Hangman was, by and large, a cheerful fellow. It was only his hood that made him seem more ominous than he really was. That and the tools of his trade. Many times he had thought of throwing it all over and becoming a fisherman. "Madam," he said to the mothers who begged him with assurances of their sons' guiltlessness, "it may be just as you say it is. I am not the judge. Merely the executioner." Once he had cut the rope on a last second pardon and that had been a wonderful day. It was fortunate that the young man had lost so much weight in prison, otherwise his neck would have been broken by the fall. "Bless you!" the young man's mother had said to him. "Have you any children of your own?" "No," the hangman admitted. "I have not. My work has taken up most of my time." "Then you can never know how much happiness you have brought me." Who says that we do not each bring a little light into the world, or what the measure is of a single deed?

Great Books. One of the great books I left unwritten (and this concerns me not just as an artist, but as a person — for art is how I explain me to myself) was derived of a sentimental condition from which I no longer suffer. Namely, the aching after the immortal that is in us as desire. The more subtle realization that comes with age is of the immortality that is in desire's transience. Which explains why certain books must be written at a certain time of life, or not at all. Oh, who was it who said to plunge into the abyss for I would not die, but never told me that action would bring me to an even more terrifying pass?

H.H. Munro. The wit of H.H. Munro (a.k.a. Saki) is a wit of prompt and savage evisceration. His works are less acts of literature than they are acts of social terrorism. "'I feel sure that the hyena has not eaten the baby,' says Mrs. Gilpet, lamely," in Munro's short masterpiece, "The Quest." "'The hyena,'" Munro's *doppelganger* Clovis replies, "'may be equally certain that it has.'" The imaginative redress of injustice is a powerful agent of psychic closure, especially in the mind of a child. Certain writers never grow up — Jonathan Swift was another — solely for this end.

Stealth. The only justification that a satirist can give for his satire is the laughter that it provokes. Those satirists who intend by their satire to overturn injustice would do well to consult their history texts on the question of revolution. "A play of wit, forsooth! But I am not done in," says the tyrant. In fact, his ire up, he calls, no doubt, for more virgins. Stealth! my friend. Stealth! If you really do suffer, like Swift, from "savage indignation."

The Satirist. The satirist feels provocation where there is none intended. "But, merely to be ignorant of one's stupidity cannot possibly be a defense, can it?" the satirist contends.

Critics. Critics are like fleas: they exist in a palpable failure of being.

Popular Wisdom. The satirist, according to the popular wisdom, is at heart a deeply unhappy person, desperately attempting to compensate for his feelings of insecurity. "But who among us would say that he is not a deeply unhappy person, desperately attempting to compensate for his feelings of insecurity?" the satirist replies. In this way, he hopes to flush out the hypocrites. That is, all those who dare respond to his query heartily or with a worked up fey diffidence.

Given this World. "If one is not deeply unhappy, one is most likely delusional," the satirist says, "given this world." But, just try to take it away from him. He will fight like a dog for even the bare bone of it. Satire is two parts pity, one part rage.

Blake. It is not as if enough has not already been written about him, but among those who have taken a crack at it, who has had sufficient quality of mind to do him justice? Algernon Charles Swinburne? Well, perhaps. But that was more than one hundred years ago. Since then, who? I ask rhetorically, of course, for I have not had time to peruse all the innumerable volumes of Blake hagiography that this century has produced. Doubtless many of them are brilliantly enlightening, as to the augury of this supreme being. But, are any of them mimetic of his essence? That, dear reader, is what

I am asking; and that is just what our literary critics so rarely provide. How could they? you may protest. They are analysands, not clairvoyants. To which I reply: a critic who is not also a clairvoyant has no business being a critic. What sense, after all, can be made of an artist's work without some glint of the soul through which it achieved its earthly registry?

His Humor. Swinburne refers to Blake's "humor" as "the cool insanity of (his) manner." To which I can only add in a more contemporaneous context that it is Zen-like. It is my firm and fond belief that Blake was more Chinese than English – in the same sense that J.D. Salinger once said of Franz Kafka that many of the passages in Kafka's *Diaries* would be suitable for "usher(ing) in the Chinese New Year." "No bird soars too high if he soars with his own wings," wrote Blake.

Women. Everywhere there are women, yet suffering men abound. Why is it not written that whoredom is sanctity? Boldly. In fact, on the very faces of the blessed angels themselves. All anguish could be ended this night. This grave be made a garden by one overturning of the moral order. The damned curse the living. That can be the only reason why this madness carries on.

Deviltry. Some have said that Blake's *Heaven and Hell* is a comic masterpiece. All genuinely prophetic works are. It takes a touch of sulfur to write them in the first place. A hint of deviltry. "The lust of the goat is the bounty of God," wrote Blake. (And who more-so than a Satyr is prepared at every moment to enter into Paradise?)

Appetite. Appetite cannot be sated until the specifics of the hunger are identified. Thus, the sole purpose of critical acumen is self-recognition, regardless of its apparent objective. The fiction, for instance, of those bloodless postmodern technicians (in their science-of-the-mind laboratories!) is often hailed as "unflinching," as though that were a virtue. In fact, it is merely an extension of the misapprehension that the possible and the necessary are indistinguishable from one another when it comes to the "artifact" of the text. In fact, the necessary is the soul of the possible. Drawing water from a dry well? Drinking sand? You know that much at least, my friends, of what satisfies and what does not.

Baudelaire's Art Writings. "Moderation has never appeared to me to be the hallmark of a vigorous artistic nature," wrote Baudelaire. And (of E.A. Poe): "Are there consecrated souls, destined for sacrifice, condemned to march toward death and glory, through the ruins of their own lives?" Perhaps the most convincing devil's advocacy since Blake's *Marriage of Heaven and Hell.* Certainly the finest critical prosody ever committed to the page, with the exception perhaps of Nietzsche's *From the Souls of Artists and Writers.* Such illustrious company he keeps – now that he is dead! – in that walled city known to us as History.

II

Old Man Winter. The thing that is hard to get used to, before experience compels one to the realization, is that there is something to everything (Christianity, Nihilism). Even the love of Old Man Winter for the buds of spring.

The Ladder. There is no final rung to the ladder. It continues on in a darkness through which (by faith or by raw courage) one must somehow counsel oneself to reach.

Enlightenment. It seems to me that one might choose, finally, the (formal) path to enlightenment, simply out of boredom with the alternatives.

Nothing. There is nothing, finally, that cannot be turned into art. In fact, there is nothing but art. Every grain of sand is potentially a pearl, until finally – satiated, overwhelmed – one seeks only to be delivered from all thought of "treasure," to a world wherein all value all things equally, as they are. Meanwhile, my friends, make no haste.

Oedipal Complex. Artistry is not all psychoanalytical in origin. Sometimes it is purely psychospiritual. So let's hear no more about how the weight of the father is borne in upon us, nor about how much protest, upon this point, is too much.

We Are. We are the habitating creatures of that relentlessly ongoing union of time, the father, and space, the mother. It's all womb, out of which there is no emergence.

Fortune. I wonder who is the luckiest person in the world? I mean, moment for moment, the one to whom the most random good fortune befalls. The one into whose lap trips the pretty girl, not once, not twice, but time and time again. The one who bends to pick the quarter, the crumpled greenback, who pulls the winning ticket from the whirling barrel, not once, not twice, but . . . And is this person aware of the vicissitudes of fortune as they pertain to him?

Humor. Humor is not contrary to any genuine religious precept. Contrary to every sentimental precept, yes, but those are not the genuine precepts of religion. Unless (as only the angels can!) you account the mediocre and the hypocrite among the blessed. You and I? Let us not deceive ourselves simply for the appearance of genuflection.

Backstage. I much prefer the back stage shenanigans, to the performance itself. A question of the Romantic versus the Classicist? Hardly! Just a personal statement of aesthetic that does not preclude, I hope, a realistic sense of any immediate, actual context or pre-existing condition. The point of artistry is not to dun one's imperative against a wall of absolute antipathy (like a dog barking against fire!) but to create a space into which the art that one most desires can be born.

Juggler. How humiliating to see him. He started out at the same time that I did. How far past me he has gone now. His skill. His repertoire. Ah, no! Even that I could stand. I could stand even that. But his beauty, no, that I cannot stand.

Failure. A colossal failure of the imagination is no less mysterious than a colossal achievement of the imagination – and no less the result of a colossal ambition.

Laughter. There is the "laughter of the damned," and then there is the damned laughter of whom J.D. Salinger referred to as "the amateur." It is this amateur laughter, rather than the mediocre clown, that is destroying comedy. Just as it is not the poor poets but incompetent readers that will eventually reduce poetry to drivel.

Breton. You get the feeling, reading Roger Shattuck's *Revolution of the Mind,* or in fact any biography of Andre Breton, that the man never laughed out of any upwelling of good humor, but always – rather – to make clear the superiority of his taste. cf. "Certain lines were singled out by Breton uniquely for their ability to make us laugh with an offensive, *wholly new* [italics mine], absolutely wild laughter."

Picasso. It is clear that Picasso was an artist who knew how to laugh. The intellectual is always afraid of the artist who truly knows how to laugh, because laughter is the one force that it is impossible to denigrate with reason.

Spontaneity. There is no theory of spontaneity in Picasso's work, there is only spontaneity. Advantage: Picasso. Breton was a control freak advocate of spontaneity. It is frequently the case that we advance the cause of freedom from that to which we ourselves are the most bound. True revolutionary freedom is expressed as indifference. What the Buddhists call "detachment." Which is why Breton was understood to unconditionally admire the ultra-diffident Duchamp.

Shattuck. Shattuck refers to Alfred Jarry as "a sensible maniac." The eventuality of a "hard-working artisan father and an unstable romantic mother." Of course, not every such coupling will produce an offspring like Jarry who at age twelve was writing "poems and skits in the style of Victor Hugo and Florian that showed unusual precociousness and merciless observation." But, let us admit, in every hundred-thousandth or millionth such pairing, it is as inevitable as, say, a birth defect. Which, in all probability, a surrealist tendency is.

Jarry. Shattuck writes: "Jarry was a mixture of vice and virtue, half brat, half prodigy – a *potache*. This *familiar* [ironic italics mine] French word for schoolboy connotes mild toleration for the frenzied play acting of adolescence [awed italics mine]. The other potache of French literature, Rimbaud, could not sustain the role. He abandoned his career as a poet at the age of 19 to become an ill-starred adventurer. Jarry died at 34 in a gradual suicide by poverty, drink, and *violated identity* [!!Italics mine]." Whatever this says about Jarry, about the trials of a poetic vocation, about the relationship of Jarry to Rimbaud, it also says (shouts!) *damn! this Shattuck can really riff!* So often between a biographer and subject, one can imagine the look of disdain that the subject might save for the biographer were they two together in time, on some alternate plane of the possible, and passed one another going opposite ways. "Suicide by Hallucination," incidentally, is the title of Shattuck's chapter on Jarry. I hope I don't have to offer any more evidence than that for their parity.

Jarry's Play. "Jarry attended several of Mallarme's Last Tuesday soirees in the *Rue de Rome* and often finished the evening alone with the poet of silence and the sonnet form." So ripe an aside, so casually tossed off, bespeaks what if not the immense range of possible topics which Shattuck had at hand? One often wishes to say, "Wait! Hold there a moment." Until one realizes how interestingly Shattuck has moved on. "The curtain rang down that night and the next on the only two performances of (Jarry's play) 'Ubu Roi.' Present in the house was a young Irishman by the name of William Butler Yeats. His description of the performance is worth repeating." Please! And, if you would, Monsieur Shattuck, do so *lingeringly.*

Jarry's Humor. "Nor was Appolinaire simply a poet who chanced to write a surprisingly sensitive book about cubism in 1913. He was a working critic of the arts," writes Shattuck. This "working" condition is probably what kept Appolinaire's "humor" "connected," in a way that you could not say – if you could even say of his "humor" that it was "humor" – of Jarry's. If Jarry's "humor" was "humor," it was "humor" of disconnection.

Personal Note. The life I have longed to lead is not available to anyone, let alone to me, but I can still dream of it, which is why the biographical excesses of Shattuck's *The Banquet Years* so appeal.

In the Final. In the final summation, Picasso was a brilliant actor playing the lifelong role of the brilliant artist. First and foremost, Picasso is a performance. Whereas with Breton, you never got the feeling that he ever believed himself to be anyone but Breton.

III

Goethe. Goethe, they say, never spent a moment of his eighty plus years not in love. At seventy-three he was writing love letters to an eighteen year old girl. The immortal Wolfgang! What then? Should I despise the same in myself as frailty? Strive to overthrow? Presume to become the master of my master?

Dylan Thomas. On almost any page of *The Collected Poems of Dylan Thomas* one can find the word "sea." Well, and what of it? Thomas was a Welshman. The sea must inhabit his imagination like the desert inhabits that of a Bedouin tribesman. No poet has ever written single more beautiful lines: "The heron priested shore." Nor painted more vibrant imagery: "The round Zion of the water bead/And the synagogue of the ear of corn." A water-colorist, really. A water-creature, for sure. How to heaven the singing blood does call, whatever object the lyric takes for its idol. That is why Oscar Wilde said there is no moral or immoral writing, there is only good writing and bad.

Shelley. Shelley's assertion that "poets are the unacknowledged legislators of the world," is usually good for a few laughs these days. What Shelley probably meant to say was that "beauty" and "power" (which at the time he wrote actually were in the hands of a few Romantic poets and which are now [ca. 2004] in the hands of young women and business magnates) are the "unacknowledged" legislative forces that "carry the day." The mistake that he made was the quite common one of mistaking the container for the thing contained. The form in which the thing is carried, for the quality that it expresses. In which case his remark is neither wrong, nor comical. Only that its "rightness" is contingent upon the moment of its utterance maintaining itself in stasis unto perpetuity. Which is just the thing that each moment cannot do. If there is a moral to be drawn from this, it is that a poet ought not to invest more energy in the object of his perception than in Perception itself, or time will make him its fool to posterity. (N.B. This goes double if you substitute the word "desire" for the word "perception.")

Gimcrack. Gimcrack religions are just fine by me. It's the impeccable cosmogonies that I can't stand.

Easy? You think it is easy? It is not so easy! Everything has to do with the first word down. I awaken, pen in hand, not knowing even what season this is.

Autobiography. No one looked with more envy than I upon the work itself. No one was less gracious in the presence of mastery. No one looked upon the sublime with more ambition. What is authorship? It is a runaway horse.

Existentially Speaking. Existentially speaking, deep artistry consists in the manifest achievement of a personal sensibility, such that from the work can be drawn answers to all questions about the author's faith. Even those that he did not address.

Tolerance. The difference between the acceptance that comes from tolerance and the acceptance that comes from insight, is the difference between sentimentality and wisdom. It is not enough to behave correctly, we must understand correctly – else one's own deeds, be they ever so auspicious, stand between one's self and one's freedom.

Elitism. A basic elitism lies within each of us, founded on the over-estimation of our individual self-worth (which is itself, likely, an aspect of the primitive instinct for survival). This basic elitism can be both misperceived as, and/or sublimated into: racism; classism; misogyny; misanthropy; and every other divisive or hierarchical self-identification or deemed identity. In fact, this elitism is merely the vanity we derive from the illusion of our uniqueness. Our vaunted individuality. True, some do will their distinction as oppositional – Ku Klux Klans-people versus the Jewish, Democrats versus the Republicans – but mostly the insult is an accidental aspect of faculties so deep rooted that one would need to attain self-mastery to transcend them. There are no individuals, of course, so there can be no distinctions to wound or be wounded by, but that is for a better world than ours to prove.

First Principle. A priest might, over a wedding couple, in the name of some Mysterious First Principle, make a solemn *pronunciemento.* However, "man and wife" is merely a lifetime contract that the eternal union of spirit and flesh as rightfully supersedes as the measure of time and space does any self-important sense of individuation in its transient masquerade of personal identity.

Bitterness. Bitterness is a clarificant. Not to be denigrated. That is why the fact of life being, from beginning to end, a bitter irony, is so deeply amusing.

Book of the Tiger

Identity. Every protestation (of identity, of philosophy) is subject to the dreary remonstrance of counterpoint. As if one were unaware that the dialectical opposition to every point is implied by the very fact of that point being made. As if one were unaware of the fact of one's own shadow. It is on this account that individuals of acute critical sensibility sometimes become Zen: that sect's recognition that the high point of rational discourse is the achievement of a logical paradox. Inarguably, the spirit of illumination is in the form of a question, but it would be less profound at this point to say, "Ah, but which question?" than it would be to fall silent.

Century after Century. Century after century passes and nothing, of course, ever changes. The souls of men and women remain at odds. Encountering one another – in this world or that – we fail the fundamental lesson of looking with our hearts through what is, in fact, the rather thin disguise of face and flesh, to the aspect at the core of Being which, like a bridge of light, unites us. We are fooled in the dark of the eyes to believe that there are distinctions – and for the sake of our desires which we dare not, at the cost of our lives, dishonor.

Means and Ends. There are means and there are ends, but there are no certain means to certain ends. It might be that this sun toward which I have set my face – this star, this bride – is already behind me. And that the wedding, too, has taken place. What need for searching? Simply to find the finger upon which to slip the ring? That token of our union? Trifles! Baubles! What are these to the eternal promise kept within us?

Fishermen. There is only one sport, really, and that is chasing around after those beings in girl-bodies. It really should be a "catch and release" sport, though. The high-minded proponents of eternal wedded bliss notwithstanding.

Moral Issues. The issues that one could call moral are in reality issues of perspective. That is, they are aesthetic issues. Life is a kinetic sculpture – not excluding, even, the ultimate mechanics of the cosmos.

Knowledge. Most of what passes for knowledge in our age is in fact merely superstition. Those cautionary tales that have been handed down through our ancestry for the seeming sole purpose of undermining the process of thought. When one is looking to the future, one must literally "give up the ghost." For instance, it is not clear to me that any inevitable harm should be wrought upon my family through my prospective carnal union with X. I am, in any case, divided-in-two, however much my longing is concealed. How should I advise my son, for instance, were he to come to me with an apple he had foresworn before he could understand what the nature of his hunger would come to be? The vows that one breaks are nothing to the ongoing maintenance of "the marriage proper." There is only one man and one woman, and that is time's body which is in space to wed. To be a priest upon an altar is too grossly to simplify the nature of understanding. In *The Book of the Tiger,* whom do you suppose it is who signifies?

Mathews. "The erotic thrall of work as a restraint against despair," writes the late poet William Matthews. But what the hell does he mean by slipping Freud in everywhere the mind has assumed its true governance? That who, after all, is trying to kid whom, herein?

Work. God, I love to work! Up at four today. All night Thursday through the late morning. Total absorption. A trance. Dear Lindsay, if there is anything in a book like the pleasures of life then this, I think, is how it is achieved. P.S. The body – its hunger unsated – translated!

Infamy. If the poet did not exist, the poetry might almost be bearable. The poems of the dead – precisely upon that principle – are preferable to the poems of the living. I shudder to think of their lives. The indolence. The infamy. And their poor, poor family members. Beholden by blood or bound by marriage. How they must have suffered to understand. Even on my own account, I can explain nothing. One mistake on the heels of another. Like two mad dogs chasing the shadow of a fox, in the silver autumn moonlit forest night.

History. The narrative of history is always ten parts romance to every part of indubitableness. Every act, in each of our lives, is aspected by the transitory connective threads of its material moment. The act, in its isolation, may even be viewed on a video tape, but its moment, in all its complex divinity, will only remain, thereby, the more invisible. Occurrence is, in a certain sense, an obfuscation.

Intent. Literary criticism is based predominately on the supposition of an intent. And all suppositions of intent are necessarily (to use the Freudian terminology) projective. Those few omniscients who do walk among us will naturally forgive – having long since foreseen – this conclusion.

Clarification. A thing is not true simply because I insist I know it to be the case. There are, however, no further impediments to communication, once this little anomaly has been redressed. The best advice that I can give is to write against type. If you are instinctively, and by ethos, a transcendentalist, attempt only satire. A horse-laugh! That more than any indignant spiritual exegesis renders a soul incorruptible.

A Complexity. A complexity of psychic and psychological conditions (some of them utterly rudimentary) make it impossible for me to give a good accounting of myself in the physically critical moment. Oh, but in the immediate aftermath, in the solitary resumption of that botched dialogue, that misplayed hand, when the Spirit of the Occasion arises from the grave of the occasion, boxed and buried and burned (in time) away, to beg my forgiveness for the clumsy materiality of its previous incarnation (that had allowed the crucial thread of Truth to be left dangling from the whole-seeming cloth of "what could be said"), I am, of course, not just vindicated, but redeemed, in the only holy righteousness a poet can allow himself to experience: that purification, through sufferance, of his art.

II

cf. Blake. The lyric engenderment of a practical sexual ecstasy is what to the bodily deed? Answer: a pathetic sublimation.

Short Takes. The energy of division/is in unity. In unity/paradox. A perfect whole/would be a perfect emptiness. Metaphysical reality is a property risen from thought, which is itself a risen property. (In fact, what is not a risen property of some great precedent? In fact, only the paradox, seeking nullity, achieves).

Of Identity. Either we create ourselves or we reveal ourselves, or there is no distinction between creation and revelation, except in the individual perception, and the paradox of identity is purely dialectical.

Sense of Proportion. "A tempest in a teapot?" Yes, well, but what is conflict based upon if not the utter lack of any sense of proportion? By which is meant, a failure to understand the real set of standards against which all is measured. "A tempest in a teapot?" Our place in the cosmos suggests that all our conflicts will ultimately be viewed as such. A speck upon which many wars were waged, cracked like a gnat on a thumbnail.

Psychoanalysis. Psychoanalysis is the new Catechism. Avoid it as you would the door of a church whose elder was not ecumenical. In Imagination is true unity.

Every Act. Every act is, in some degree, a commentary on the act which preceded it. An act which bears no relation to the act which preceded it is a theoretical ideal toward which something called "pure creativity" might aspire, but which as yet (sorry Dada, Surrealism, Post-modernism) is beyond us. And it will remain beyond us so long as conscious effort continues to be made toward its achievement. What might happen, though, how a "pure creativity" might come about: it might need us, as the medium of its own desire to achieve itself. I personally believe this is what will happen, because all things that are possible must inevitably occur. Even if only in a state analogous to that sound which a tree makes falling in the forest when there is nobody to hear it. In which case, despite our failed efforts to bring it about, it may already have occurred.

Dragon. It is easier for me, I suppose, to look through the behaviors into the conditions out of which they arise because I have a motivation for doing so: the art dragon has got to be fed – and after all these years of being the spoiled kept pet (of Messrs. Picasso, Keats, etc.) only the eternal verities will serve. That is to say: it is not a dog-meat situation when one takes on the responsibilities of such a guardianship.

Some Hubris. If one were to lack a facility for language, one might make of that lack of facility a point of honor, as though it were a choice, rather than a condition of limitation. So, too, one who lacked a capacity for insight.

Peter Cook and Dudley Moore. "Have you learned from your mistakes?" "Yes, I have learned from my mistakes and I believe that I could repeat them exactly." That is a bit written by Cook and Moore back in the early 1960s . What they mean by "timeless comedy." That is, a joke based not in transient cultural verities, but in eternal human verities. The roots of the comic impulse are founded in a psychic capaciousness that does not lend itself easily to critical analysis. In this sense, the comic gift and the mystic gift (cf. Blake) are close aligned.

More Eros. I do not say that Eros is a false friend, but perhaps a too fair-weather one.

Will. Is the power of Will more mysterious than the hand of God?

World. A tiered system upon a tilting sphere. How stable could it be?

Duty. The artist enters upon himself as upon an uncharted territory, casting aside all self-knowledge as the original crown of thorns.

Dreaming. The thing about dreaming is there is always an exit. From being awake, there is no exit. There is a door for departure, but that is not the same thing. One does not often return to the same dream (though victims of trauma might argue this), but day after day the same life recurs. The question of how to live is wrapped up in the question of whether or not it is possible to awaken inside one's own life as the lucid dreamers are said to awaken inside their dreams. And if an awakening within a state of awakedness is possible – that is, to put it romantically – if our life is but a dream, then upon that life, what measure of control ought we to be able to exert?

About. It is not about anything. It is not even about oneself. It is simply an admixture of gestures, half formed, half flung, from some orbiting center in fealty to some ever-deepening gravity which has, as its source, an inverse physics so absolute as to deny even the notion of structure.

Children. It is so important to children that their greetings and leave-takings be seriously engaged. That their absences be remarked upon, as if without their presence there was something less to the circumstance than there ought to have been. Children who are not given to feel themselves important will try to impress their importance on the world by one means or another. On the one hand, by creative means: art, music, performance; on the other hand, by destructive means: murder, assault, treachery. It is all in the formation of internal resources, where these outlets have their origin. And is there any one of us who would not sacrifice all art, all performance, all music, if it meant the end, as well, of murder, assault, treachery? This sounds simple and it is simple. The question of human evolution and of individual happiness is always determined by the simplest measures.

Rocks. The rocks rolled smooth by breaking waves are like memories rolled smooth in a tide of narration drawn by the moon of the Will.

Beautiful. It is one thing to be romantic on another's account, or in execution of some behest, but the Self must be a stone against which the seas bash furiously to no avail. All of us will become more beautiful, finally, when we are absent. If there is an explanation for this, it may be found in the characterization of individual Will, however well intended, and of personality, however heroically resolved, as "over-determined."

Athletics. The thing about athletics as opposed to intellectuality, as a competitive enterprise, is at least there is no delusion in sports that one person is as good as the next. One can always say of the betterness or worseness of a poem that it is all subjective, but you cannot say of the one who has run the 500 meter dash in one minute flat that his victory over the one who ran it in one minute and seven seconds is all subjective. This is obvious and should go without saying, but it is a point of particular irritation to somebody like myself, leading a life of the intellect, and watching those whose poems have, in effect, run the 500 meters in a minute and a half be touted as the victors over those whose poems are clearing the same distance in the blink of an eye. There should be a purely objective method for evaluating works of art, an unassailable criterion – and there is. It is called History. But doubtless this is of as little solace to the post-humous as it is to the pre-.

III

All Your Science. "Who is this paradise? A woman, no doubt? A girl? Extraordinary. A girl. Simply that. And all things are there with her? The garden? The delight? Extraordinary. Mysterious. Magical. All your science will not do for you what she can? Amazing! Preposterous! Confounding!"

Dissertation. James is writing his doctoral dissertation on Heavy Metal Rockers as the New Dionysians. "Their revels, let's face it," he says, "have the transmoral quality of divine inspiration. Of being, in the lyrical, Nietzschean sense, beyond good and evil. That is why we do not begrudge them their escapades or think any the less of them. They are drinking from the pure river of desire. Life's unstopped essence. Like infants at the breasts of their mothers, they know only the power of thirst and the immoderacy of fullness that derives from its conquest. Of course," he adds, shaking his head, "you would not want your sister to be deflowered by one of them." "Oh, no, indeed," I reply, heartily.

My Desk. My desk is a stage, whereupon I perform – as it were – between the acts of thinking, the masquerade of thought. My life is a stage, whereupon I perform – as it were – between the acts of living, the masquerade of consciousness.

Imagination. I guess it's true. I do live in my imagination. "In my mind," as they say – but not deep in my mind. "Do you even realize that there is anything out there?" I am sometimes asked. Meaning: beyond the boundaries of myself. This impossible naïve question can only be answered if one feigns entire innocence of its implications. I was raised not just in a culture of generalized post-modernism, but in a locus of its concentration. My dear, would you have me turn away from the very tenets upon which my identity was founded? The universality of the individual? Simply because there is no certitude of the range of its effects? My dear, there is no certitude in anything. Not even that when you have staunched a blood flow and breathed life back into a dying man, you have not damned an entire civilization. Causality. Is there anything more innocent than to believe that one thing must inevitably lead to the next? When on every occasion, at some point, the chain flies apart, chaos enters in, and corruption?

Profound. Great poets are all philosophers too profound to systematize their ideologies. Inside every dark visionary is a being of insidious reason waiting patiently for his host to die. From the cleft of the creative arises the categorical flower.

Method. In my writing, I am not attempting to convey the objective truth of a given situation. Rather, I am trying to convey the "energy" of the "presence" of that situation. If, in doing so, I am able to incorporate bits and pieces of that objective material of which the "reality" of that situation is (in a certain sense) constituted, I do not hesitate to do so. But, never at the cost of obstructing the ultimate intention of the piece, which is (in every case!) to celebrate the passions of the Life Force itself, and not any (mere) particular instance of that force. The mistake that I will never make as a writer is to imagine that the reader (for any good reason) ought to be able to see through the poem into the inspiration for its creation. It ought to be (if any ought to be there ought be, at all) all contained immediately therein: from the conceptual impetus to its formal culmination. This is simply the minimal deference that one makes to posterity in return for the prospect of its favors.

Zookeeper's Assistant. I worked one summer as a zookeeper's assistant, but I was forced to resign. Why? I do not recall. Some conflict or other. The elephants whom I tended were especially grieved to see me go. They trumpeted "Taps" for me, from behind the bars of their cages, as I departed. There is no escape from slavery, of course, but there is a certain illusion of freedom which we all crave. Where master and slave share the same objective. What lovers possess in the perfect carnal bed. A relationship of give and take in which the ultimate goal is mutually desired. In that moment of perfection, when nothing of ourselves remain, who cares which is the horse and which the rider? The elephant thrashing in the web of the spider.

Broken. White feather (mist on the lake, soft). Must watch my breath, not get carried away. (Moonsense). A thin white line is broken upon the water.

Camels. Three camels in the desert (words, rain, words) can live forever, eating each other (the alphabet, cannibalism).

Moon. Close her eyes with petals, fill her keyhole with water, carry her away on a silver spoon. Moon (deluxe edition) ray falls. Day could not find her, night redeems. Little rivers of the moon (dreams).

Rules. There are no rules for art, except the rule of contradiction which states: if it was true for your last piece, it is probably untrue for this one.

Books. I suppose that I love books. A good deal of my time has been spent in their midst, and I dare say a good deal more will be spent, before a period is put on the end of my sentence. I suppose I care more about textual cohesion than about the development of character. More about the rudiments of form, than about the manifest registrations of psyche that imply a revelatory contiguity. We know what might be the motivation of authorship to over-arch itself, but what might be the motivation of language to over-arch itself? In the first place, the expansion of understanding, but what in the second place? The expansion of meaning?

The Sublime. Professor so-and-so tried to teach me The Sublime as a honeyed principle of rhetoric. Now he is a petty administrator swept up in the maelstrom of academia, while I sit upon the roof of his institution like I have descended here, hurling wickedly apt epithets. Not out of any particular spite, mind you, but out of lyric excess. "Hey, blockhead!" I shout. "Where are all your debutant balls now, huh? It turns out that I was Cinderella. What do you think of that, you fairy Goddamn mother? The dance hall is wherever I put my feet. And that spinning orb overhead? A gift from my father. He runs the flipping joint. Not your 'towering dead' with their 'nightingales and psalms,' but some thick-tongued lung-fish, abiding in his hold. The Sublime, indeed! No golden world at all. A turtle, rather, dragging his heels into the fundament to stay the furious coursers. Bridles of mud upon fire-snorting horses."

The Heart of Animals. Innocent as a deer. That is a funny way of saying it. How can anything be known of the human heart? A girl: every morning she goes into the woods. No one knows what she does there. Perhaps she has a lover among the deer. Satisfied and happy, she returns each evening home and sleeps peacefully. Should all the deer be killed on account of a few disgruntled would-be-lovers? It is not right, they say, that such a mystery should attend her. A tearing off of the veil is all they wish to accomplish. It would surprise them to learn that the hearts of human beings and the hearts of animals are almost exactly formed alike.

Selfish. Each of us is selfish in exact proportion to the amount of betrayal — real or imagined — that we have experienced. Our seriousness arises from the delusion that our thoughts have meaning. These delusions are exacerbated by a tendency to assess their "meaning" by their "purchase."

Routine. Saddest thing in the world. This guy dies. He's got no relatives. He's got no friends. The authorities come and start combing through his apartment and they find boxes of these jokes that he has written. Great jokes. Brilliant jokes. That nobody has ever seen. Saddest thing in the world, all that untapped laughter. I can hardly stand even to imagine it. I could have used some of those jokes, you know. I could use one of them right now. It's tragic when a guy like me has to sit here night after night with nothing, and here's a guy throwing diamonds down a well. It all went at an estate auction for two bucks, by the way. Some illiterate machine worker bought them up as scrap paper for his juvenile delinquent son to use in making spit wads. I hope in the afterworld the dead guy is getting a real kick out of all this. I guess what I mean is that I hope the joke is not on him.

IV

Patronage. The dubious honor of our company is offset by what? The even more dubious prospect of anything like pleasure ever deriving from it? I pity the poor patron who, out of sheer idealism, mistakes the artist as someone worthy of the grandeur of the art.

Paranoia. A paranoid is someone whose ideas are controlling him, rather than the other way around. In that sense, much of political discourse could be called paranoid. Henry Miller referred to Rimbaud's writing method as "ambulatory paranoia." The paranoid functions predominately as creative. That is to say, predominately in the form of a narrative. This does not mean that all narrative is paranoid. On the other hand, the component of paranoia at work, say, in the narratives of Dostoyevsky cannot be underestimated.

Schizophrenia. Take the case of Artaud. Without his schizophrenia, we would not have his, "Umbilicus of Limbo," although, I am speaking solely of that essay's incommensurable title and not of its unintelligible content. The schizophrenic may possess genius, but rarely any sense of weight or measure.

Mania. Well, Sinclair Lewis, Robert Lowell. I do not think there is a near end to the list of writers who moved through creativity on the wings of their mania. In fact, of any of us artist types, in the right (or should one say, the wrong) context, it might be noted on a physician's chart: mania! and underscored twice in red-ink.

Depression. Kurt Vonnegut wrote that as far as he could determine, the common denominator among the world class novelists who were his contemporaries (Styron, Boll, etc.), was that they were all depressives who came from families of depressives. I believe this was expressed as a mordancy.

Connotative and Denotative. "Every woman loves a brute," wrote Sylvia Plath. And every reader, too. The virtue of the denotative is that it takes into account actual conditions, while the connotative presumes upon an ideal that has never yet materialized. Men and women are creatures of psychology, upon the brows of whom, occasionally, the shadow of a dancing star falls. It is the madness of the connotative dictum that these dancing star moments are the true defining moments of our nature. If there is a commensurate madness in the denotative dictum, it resides not in the dict-um, but in the dict-or. That is to say, it is the speaker who might cling to the spoken, but the spoken itself, whatever the seeming authority of its tone or address, through the realization of its potency, has already begun its translation.

Desolation. There are no degrees of desolation, really. There is only desolation. It is just as the poet Lorna Dee Cervantes says of genocide. That it does not deconstruct.

An Essay on the Essay. An essay is not simply a pile of sentences nailed together willy-nilly, any more so than a house is a pile of planks nailed together willy-nilly. It is not enough that the vestige of form is maintained such that from a distance, in the dark, the shadowy outline of what may, indeed, be a house can be discerned. It is a question of whether or not, in the harsh glare of daylight, after stepping through the entryway, anyone of sound mind would gladly choose to live in it. And of essays, if – in the harsh absence of a vested interest (such as a teacher with her red pen, or a doting parent, might have) – after reviewing the opening sentences, anyone would greedily pursue the engagement.

Twilight. "Fifty or sixty," says the poet Petger Schaberg "Even seventy. It is never too late." "What about ninety?" I ask. "What about one hundred?" "Never!" Schaberg insists. "It is never too late." But the truth is that from the moment we are born it is already too late. Far, far too late (the twilight!) for any of us.

The World. It is reassuring to realize that the world is larger than we are, and that, commensurately, the idea is always larger than the mind that attempts to conceive of it. If we are rooted, we are rooted from every cell of our being, and if we are rooted from every cell of our being then there is a foundation, a grounding, for every aspect of that of which we are composed. And for every one of those groundings, for every one of those foundations, a concurrent ceiling, a concurrent sky.

The Eternal Present. The philosophy of The Eternal Present purveyed egoistically (cf. Wordsworth) is not the philosophy of The Eternal Present purveyed Buddhistically. The intention of the former is revolutionary, the intention of the latter is sanguinary: a matter of making the peace within oneself. The Buddhist spirit is almost invariably corrupted by externalization, which is to say: the eternal Tao is not the Tao that can be told. A lantern lit in a cavern, it is true, illuminates only that cavern. Has this any virtue? Answer: It eases the moment's suffering. But, has this any virtue? Answer: No, no virtue. Are there selfless acts of compassion? Answer: Are there selfless acts of indifference?

A Sentence. A sentence is not a puzzle to be figured out, unless there is a specific reason for creating it as such: you have an opinion, for instance, about the oppressive paradigm that grammar has become; or, you believe that there is beauty in the strange; or, there is an underlying musical structure, or rhythmic structure that you are building upon; and so forth. These are the kinds of issues that artists tend to obsess upon and to present for engagement. That is to say, if you are working as an artist then you may grant yourself a certain amount of leeway in your sentence constructions. However, if you are not working as an artist (and this can only be known to yourself, in your deepest heart of hearts), then do not ask of your reader what the artist asks.

Portrait. Pat is a mystery. If you look in his eyes, one thing you never see is fear. But, it is not, either, that he projects self-assurance. There is simply some kind of a stillness there. The stillness, perhaps, of one who is working in his mind to unlock a puzzle. It would be easy to make fun of Pat. All those who have sold themselves into the slavery of the creative are innately laughable. We live in a universe divinely created. Above us, spheres in orbit around one another extend beyond the mind's ability to fathom. At the bottom of the ocean there are sightless fish that live whole, full lives, in their caves. There is the persimmon, and the artichoke. There is the Narwhale, the butterfly. There is the miraculous profusion of spring. There is the searing and melancholy decline of autumn. There is you and there is me: the complex of our design – interior and exterior. For anyone who has looked at the world as a precision-made object layered over with beauty of every order, the idea of a human-made creative construct can pall into a laughable insignificance. On the other hand, my friends, in lieu of our ephemeral condition. In lieu of the transient nature of our very being, what activity is not, somehow, laughable?

Someone's Biography. Someone somewhere will publish a book of your poetry and thirty or so people will read it and you will convince yourself that those are the only thirty people who matter. Perhaps it will be one of those thirty people to whom you get married and from whom, several years later, you get divorced without having had any children. "Our poems will be our children," you will have told one another, during the glory days when the sex was still propitious. The tragedy of your life will not come clear to you even then and perhaps a second book will follow the first, attended by appointment to the English department of a small East-coast college. There you will spend several years trying to write a novel, but it is not so easy to write a novel and you will concede a grudging admiration for those "hacks who just bash it out, without regard for the music of language." Your second marriage will be to a successful novelist whose star will shine so much brighter than yours that when he abandons you in a few years no one will be surprised. Your next failed attempt will be at memoir. At this point, the tragedy of your life, which had long been evident to everyone else will finally become evident to you. There will be pills and younger men and an attempted suicide. Followed by a third, critically acclaimed, book of poetry, which will give you no greater connection to a large world than did either of the first two, critically disregarded. Meanwhile you will have been granted tenure. You will have given several dozen sparsely attended readings. You will be in touch across computer wires with a group of like-minded poets whose straits are similar to your own and on whose good opinions of you you must continue to rely, having no longer recourse to any of your own. The fire you had set to blaze forever has now burned out.

Cunning and Clarity. The artist must be careful on the one end to avoid corruption, and on the other, disenfranchisement. Corruption in art means that the artist is working out of a bias or premeditation. That is to say, the artist is working so willfully as to preclude the advent of the unconscious. In disenfranchisement, the artist spends the time that ought to be spent on the art in maintaining personal stasis: food, shelter, creature comforts, companionship. Unless born rich or lucky, an artist must take the measure of his or her prospects and work within them in order to forge a lifestyle that allows both the freedom and the security necessary to continue working, experimenting, and evolving as an artist over the course not just of months or years, but of decades. An artist, that is to say, must not only maintain purity of heart, but, also: cunning. (Or, to state it in a less fractious term: clarity.)

Pope. Pope said (not the Pope; the poet, Alexander Pope): "I would never even sit down to a meal without some kind of a strategy." My friend Fred Baca said, similarly: "We're all just dogs. Either you dominate them, or they will dominate you." Women weave mysteries around the heads of those whom they bed. That bright halo of enigma that allows them to justify their submission as a way of knowing.

Book of the Tiger. All we have is what we allow ourselves to have. All we are is what we allow ourselves to be. Moral inhibitions are creations of a self in fear of its own expansion.

A Shimmer of Veils. All those unfulfilled fantasies of desire that *he* has revolved around *her*, like a shimmer of veils – what if they were transferred to someone else? – to someone willing? Would there be any reason at all ever again to even think of *her*? What becomes of those selves we have invested, when those into whom we have invested them depart? It is a matter of whether or not we still have any connection to those investments. The tragic widower knows this in one way, the gay divorcee in another.

Hamsun. The early lyric manner (Pan, Mysteries, etc.) threads it way through all the middle and late period works (Women at the Pump, Wayfarers, etc.) energizing the resignation of the former and humanizing the profundity of the latter.

Understanding. It is a mistake to imagine that philosophical recognition equates to understanding, or even that philosophical recognition is a step on the road to understanding. In fact, understanding, if it is to make any impact at all, must precede philosophy. Who does not believe this must ask himself if it is impossible for the seed to burst simply because it does not know that it is to become a flower.

We Must. We must raise ourselves up, as the habit of rising perpetuates itself.

A Useful Thinker. A useful thinker is one who, in the balance, appraises his virtue as about the equal of his vice. It is no use to think as either a god or a devil, if the point is to clarify what it means to be a human being. So much of our own humanity is lost to us in trying to think thoughts that are not actually our own, in the misguided sense that such thoughts must be better than the ones that do possess us. Better thoughts, worse thoughts, what can their promise be for our eventual "self-actualization," if the mind that understands them is not our own?

Survival Mode. I am in "survival mode." Right! It is not a matter of waiting for things to improve. It is a matter of continuously drawing back close those things that are continuously slipping away. There are details, but the details are not the issue. The issue is survival. The issue is drawing back close those things that are slipping away. This may be (though I do not desire it) the condition of my life from now, forever after. Or it may be that tomorrow larks will fly and the face of the sky break into a wide smile.

Genius v. Logic. One arrives at genius by following genius and genius has not the same restrictions upon its passage as has logic. Logic takes into account all those edicts that fall under the category of "cautionary." Genius knows only that it is born to die.

Those Demons. People say, "The demons that drove his comedy," or "demons that drove his poetry," but what about the demons that drive a fellow to clerk at a hardware store, year after year, or to remain married to a spouse who has become, effectively, a stranger, or those other demons, the ones who bring you in chains to pay obeisance at the altar of Aphrodite.

Advice to Aspirants. Leave out all the uninteresting bits.

Publication. Most writing does not matter, from the moment that it is written. Publication, even awards, cannot change what – time after time – time proves. But there is that beaming moment of achievement, and that cannot be taken away from the achiever. Just as the lover who "made hay" only because he came in the darkness and was mistaken for another, cannot have the moans of that union taken away.

Warmth. So much of wit and insight, warmth and humor are the result of dereliction – in the sense that dereliction must seek, eventually, to be redeemed.

Coda

A pure, unadorned idea. Some may achieve its adumbration. However, the shadow of a pure, unadorned idea is not the pure, unadorned idea itself. Unless it is the perfect shadow (which cannot fall!) of the immaterial essence (from which it cannot be cast!) of a pure, unadorned idea. Is there such a thing, then, as the "close enough" representation of a pure, unadorned idea? Or is everything that is not "it, exactly," an obfuscation? Beauty, for example. Can one be in a nightmare of beauty? Can the horse over-ride itself? Objects of desire in the mirror of the river: repeat.

The quicker you come to the point, the sooner it unravels.

About the Author

Alex Stein is the author of *Dark Optimism,* a book of short fictions, and *The Life and Art of Josan,* a collection of drawings inhabited by poems. He came to the vocation of writing first as a newspaper columnist, mostly documenting the bohemian milieu of artists and zealots of that time. He holds a Ph.D. in Literature from the University of Denver, an honor he achieved too far along in life for it to have given him much sense of personal achievement, but an experience of institutionalized scholarship that, unlike previous ventures into academia, offered him much in the way of illuminated moments, and of fundamentally sane human interaction: two things for which he is always, anytime, and anywhere he encounters them, a surprised and grateful recipient. He makes his living working for a university library in Boulder, Colorado, where he has lived and sometimes even thrived, for 25 years. He has two children, boys, whose characters he very much encourages and admires.

Wings Press was founded in 1975 by Joanie Whitebird and Joseph F. Lomax, both deceased, as "an informal association of artists and cultural mythologists dedicated to the preservation of the literature of the nation of Texas." The publisher/editor since 1995, Bryce Milligan is honored to carry on and expand that mission to include the finest in American writing, without commercial considerations clouding the choice to publish or not to publish. Technically a "for profit" press, Wings receives only occasional underwriting from individuals and institutions who wish to support our vision. For this we are very grateful.

Wings Press attempts to produce multicultural books, chapbooks, CDs, DVDs and broadsides that, we hope, enlighten the human spirit and enliven the mind. Everyone ever associated with Wings has been or is a writer, and we know well that writing is a transformational art form capable of changing the world, primarily by allowing us to glimpse something of each other's souls. Good writing is innovative, insightful, and interesting. But most of all it is honest.

Likewise, Wings Press is committed to treating the planet itself as a partner. Thus the press uses as much recycled material as possible, from the paper on which the books are printed to the boxes in which they are shipped.

Associate editor Robert Bonazzi is also an old hand in the small press world. Bonazzi was the editor / publisher of Latitudes Press (1966-2000). Bonazzi and Milligan share a commitment to independent publishing and have collaborated on numerous projects over the past 25 years. As Robert Dana wrote in *Against the Grain*, "Small press publishing is personal publishing. In essence, it is a matter of personal vision, personal taste and courage, and personal friendships."

Welcome to our world.

Colophon

This first edition of *Weird Emptiness: Essays & Aphorisms,* by Alex Stein, has been printed on 70 pound non-acidic paper containing fifty percent recycled fiber. Titles have been set using Skia type; the text in Caslon. The first 10 signature sets to be pulled from the press have been numbered and signed by the author. This volume was edited by Robert Bonazzi. Wings Press books are designed by Bryce Milligan.

Wings Press
www.wingspress.com
Distributed to the trade by the
Independent Publishers Group
www.ipgbook.com